GRIEF'S CHILD

THE UPS AND DOWNS AND ALL AROUNDS OF LOVE, LOSS, AND LIFE

GRETA WOOLLEY

CONTENTS

Paperback ISBN 979-8-9926505-2-5
Ebook ISBN 979-8-9926505-3-2

For all of us who have ever felt alone with our grief— This book is meant to hold you. May you find some comfort and assurance in the knowledge that others deeply care. The light is waiting on the other side for you.

There are some things you can't write about
until you have lived it so intensely,
that even your bones know it.

YOU ARE NOT ALONE

I'll never forget the most defining moment of my life.

It was my senior year of college. I had been pulling multiple all-nighters, writing twenty-page papers and studying for final exams, consuming countless pots of coffee to fuel my fire. I felt invincible, riding the high that comes when you are quickly approaching celebratory occasions such as graduation.

Mine stood two weeks away, attracting me like a magnet toward the invitation proclaiming, "Your Life is About to *Really* Start—And It's Gonna Be Great!"

Despite the illusion that life was stressful, in retrospect it was the simplest of times. Comprised of the perfect mixture of adrenaline, excitement, belief, anticipation, and ignorance, I curled up against my notebooks, ignited by the completion of tasks that brought me closer to the finish line, my commencement from the University of Florida.

It felt so big.

It felt so special.

It felt so happy.

It felt so hopeful.

And then it happened.

The phone rang.

"Is this Greta Howell?"

"Yes, it is."

"This is Deputy Miller from the Clearwater Police Department. How old are you?"

"Twenty-two," I reply, wondering who the hell this is and why he wants to know my age.

"Then, your brother must have been older than you."

"*Must* have been?"

He proceeds to inform me that there has been a terrible accident. My parents, lost in an abyss of shock, are unable to find the strength to call, so he does.

"You'll probably want to head home, now."

I try with all my might to respond, but the words just don't come.

Is this what they call traumatic mutism?

Am I already avoiding more distress by ceasing all communication?

If I silence the noise, will it change the truth of what I just heard?

Honestly, I don't even remember what happens next.

All I know is that I'm now staring into the oval-shaped mirror that hangs directly above my phone, watching my mascara melt upon my face dissolving into a tributary of dark, emotional creeks drowning my vocal cords and leading to my broken heart. I literally sit without speaking for the next hour, paralyzed in my own head.

An accident? Hurry home? I question myself. *Did I hear him right or am I dreaming?*

Phone drops.

Silence sears.

Intense heat begins to scorch my innocent blueprint for living as I watch it go up in flames.

*My life will **never** be the same.*

I arrive home to find my mother beating her fists upon my

father's chest, following the news that my brother has been ejected from his car by the sudden impact of a head-on collision with a semi-truck.

In the blink of an eye, my brother was *gone.*

"Bring him home!" my mother cries as her own mind begins to slowly slip into a parallel universe that steals her away from my screaming heart.

My God—she's gone, too! I realize.

The mother that I need to lean upon disappears into a timeless vacuum of despair, and I spend the next several years standing alone, afraid to tell anybody what I am feeling. Unsure how to construct a story that conveys the narrative called my life, I hide behind an exhausting schedule, fleeing from any real feelings that might force me to process what took place.

I begin to blindly reinforce this crazy notion that I have to hold the weight of my secrets in lonesome corners meant for mourners, never exposing to others the truth of my traumatic loss.

Oh, how I dream I could go back and comfort the younger version of myself. Her struggling brain had no idea that other people existed to comfort and support her, to teach her and talk to her, to sit still with her and lovingly lead her to higher ground.

No, *she sat alone,* convincing herself that if she didn't talk about it, the grief would somehow magically disappear.

What she didn't know then is that she would be writing this book over thirty-five years later to let others know that they never need to stand alone in their grief.

She had no notion of the prevalence of grief and the many masks grief wears.

If only one person had been able to share this powerful thought with her, perhaps she could have given herself more grace. She needed to know:

> ***Your helpers are waiting.***
> ***We can do this together.***

I was so naïve to the breadth of grief. I was an infant in my knowledge of its complexities. May this story reveal the well-needed fact that the multi-layers of loss can leave us feeling frozen in our own pain, until at last the sun begins to melt away our despair. All our stories are real. And worthy. And inclusive. And deserving of love and attention.

This book is for the families who have lost a child. A man living with suicidal thoughts at the lowest point possible after losing his job—or more, his belief in himself. Your sister or friend who got divorced after thirty years of marriage, grieving the loss of what should have been. The teenager who overdoses. The woman aching to have a baby, but the baby just doesn't come.

The Grief we meet when we lose a sibling at a young age, leaving us longing in our later years for what our "grown up" relationship might have been. The senior in high school who has been told they are not good enough to be accepted to college, so they stop setting goals. The young couple who experiences the loss of a baby through miscarriage.

Your first friend who leaves this earth long before her time due to some insane diagnosis. The feeling of being lost in a workplace that doesn't fulfill your dreams and believing that something has died inside of you. The educators, parents, and students who have experienced the horror of school violence.

The accident that creates physical limitations for your otherwise strong body and mind. Feeling the hand of the man or woman who stood beside you for the last 50 years slip away into the heavens. Your 97-year-old Grammy who, no matter how amazing and long her life was, you just weren't ready to see her pass. The sudden death from a car crash. The long goodbye of Alzheimer's. The aftermath of cancer. The parent who went to the hospital for hip surgery and was supposed to come home on Friday, but they didn't.

The best friend who moved away. Injured relationships. The feeling of being orphaned with the passing of your second parent. A pandemic named Covid sweeping the world. The abusive relationships that imprison us, causing our minds to feel trapped and alone. The voices in your head that tell you nobody cares. Mental illness.

Terrorism. Hatred. The excruciating pain that comes with being taken advantage of or neglected. Your dog or your cat passing away. The little boy in elementary school who wants to be a little girl. Lost dreams.

The person who will never understand how the color of their skin, the sound of their language, the shape of their body, the person they love, or the preference of their politics precludes them from privilege. The house or career choice you couldn't keep because of economics.

Your untold story.

This book is for you.

It's for all of us as a reminder that we are in this together.

My dear reader,

I *promise* you,

You are not alone.

MY PRAYER FOR YOU

Come, dear reader, and rest your weary head.
Lean into my body and just let yourself "go."
Let us be portals for receiving the power
of healing.
You've been holding it in for so long,
but you don't have to anymore.
I'm giving you permission to breathe.
Let the tears roll freely.
Feel your soul tremble if need be.
I'm here for you,
a warm and firm embrace
ready to rock the stories that illustrate your life:
the words, phrases, and vignettes that speak your
name.
I am just a woman.
Just an ordinary woman who knows what you are
feeling
because I have felt it too.
I want to know the intricacies of how you feel,
because who am I to tell you what your story is?

*And maybe if we share our experiences, comfort will
    envelope both of us.*
Come, take my hand,
*and let me gently guide you into the "club" you never
    wanted to join.*
I never wanted to join it, either.
But here we are, interlocked,
equipping ourselves to navigate these stormy waters
laden with generational trauma and ships of sorrow,
*with their cargo of grief, sailing in and out of our
    lives.*
Sit in my circle, ready to heal your aching wounds.
We'll rise slowly in unison.
Guided by the angels who have flown before us,
our arms linked like chains that cannot be broken
in our ascension to nurse our suffering hearts.
Let us feel our strength.
*Daily we execute the tasks supporting the
    nourishment and sustenance*
of our families, friendships, homes, and work life.
*Love, compassion, and connection run through our
    veins.*
Let us live for purpose.
*An indescribable light illuminates the challenges
    before us.*
*At times, we are distracted and discouraged by the
    universal downfalls that greet us all, but together
    we find hope as we remind each other that the
    glow awaits at every turn.*
Like gifted mathematicians,
*together we begin to calculate the possibilities of
    minimizing the dark moments*
while at the same time letting each other just...

feel *and* be *all that we are.*

We graph the probability of light overshadowing
> *dark.*

We lean into our convictions.

We openly feel all emotions without shame,

without guilt,

without confusion or excuses, apologies or
> *reluctance,*

without timelines.

We flat-out fall apart together and call upon our
> *people to aid us*

in the re-assemblance of "better versions of
> *ourselves"*

as many times as possible!

As many times as needed to be found in this
> *continuous*

rebirth and celebration called life.

Let us feel immeasurable meaning and
> **faith until our last breath.**

And then, may we be born again.

HER NAME WAS GRIEF

Thrown off at first
By smoky air
Her presence
Brings great despair—
But look deeper
And you will see
She is actually
Meant to be
Your blanket:
Weighing down
The pain you feel
Until at last
The cover falls
And with it,
All the broken walls
That kept you from the light...
Her purpose now within your sight.

MEET MY FRIEND, GRIEF

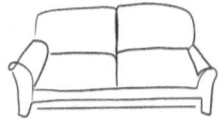

This book is about grief, the ultimate quick-change artist, who introduced herself to me at a very early age, ripping off her multiple layers of clothing to reveal her true colors. She is gruff and intolerable, but she can also be oddly loving and wise. She likes to show up at the most obvious moments but also has a knack for sneaking inside small unguarded entry points like a moody ninja warrior employing her deception.

She's not the person you want to invite to a party, but she ends up being the only one who can fully lead you to acceptance, peace, and understanding. Though it may seem strange, her love runs deeper than the ocean. You secretly hate her for what she knows, while she skillfully becomes your only true friend when you have lost someone or something that holds all your heart.

Frankly, she's the only one who really gets the difference between mourning and grieving. At first, she fights like the devil to capture your unbearable pain, offering the lock that will guard your ability to love freely again. Eventually, though, like all good friends, she leads you to higher ground—which, in this situation, happens to be the place where grieving intersects with mourning, and your feelings begin to pour out in all the right directions, your MapQuest for new possibilities. Ultimately, she convinces you that you have a capacity for giving and trusting and loving again.

Why is Grief so important to me? I know her quite well, as you will discover with the unfolding of my stories. Her refusal to pass me by persuaded me to reconsider her friendship instead of viewing her as the "mean girl" out to hurt me.

Surprisingly, behind her hidden curtains, she orchestrates some of the best life lessons. Lessons I have embraced, I must say. Ones that have defined the word *agony* for me, but also those that have allowed me to recognize my greatest joys and most abundant blessings.

If you are holding this book right now, reading my words, welcome to the club. I wish I could squeeze your hand in person and say to you, "I am sorry." Because I am so sorry for what you are going through and what you have lost. But my hope for you? I pray that you have begun a journey of healing, and I long to be a small part of helping with that. My wish is that you surround yourself with healers, lovers, understanders, empathizers, feelers, laughers, and mirrors. I'm not sure if any of us ever feel "ready" to begin this transformation in understanding. The road waits for us, carving out a million different pathways forward. Look for the hands capable of lifting you to this love-filled place and take all the time you need to begin placing one foot in front of the other.

You will need your people to do this thing. And also, you will need to do it solo much of the time. None of us will really understand what you alone must feel right now, but we will try with all our hearts.

For me, understanding Grief has been a decades-long journey. I'm still working on it, but I have become clear about some aspects. For starters, there is no right or wrong way to grieve. No timelines exist to get you through a magical sequence of events that will bolt you to a finish line. Your dearest friends and loved ones will grapple with the process alongside you, unsure what to do or say, but that doesn't mean they don't care. They will unknowingly leave you feeling abandoned at times.

I hope this book will help you to tell them what you need, because finding your voice will aid you in your journey. Your voice can be expressed in many different fashions and varied levels of volume.

While grieving, you may vacillate between the two most connected feelings on the planet: love and hate. Don't beat yourself up for that—or others. At times you will blankly stare into the universe, trying desperately to care about anything. You may even decide that you're not too fond of living, period. Managing the confusion can feel so hard at this time. Grief cloaks herself in trickery that leaves you incessantly questioning the meaning of your existence.

You will find that Time is your other dearest and most trusted companion. You won't want to believe him, but he knows about the passage of life and the comfort that comes after one second has turned into one year and so forth. He will get on your nerves at times. He might try to talk you into doing things that you are not ready for. Just be honest with him, and you will be fine. You do not have to act to please him by rushing the process. Be open to his loving push, though. He may illuminate and accelerate your growth when least expected. Pay attention to the signs.

If you are anything like me, you may sob in one second and in the next find yourself becoming a master at compartmentalizing your feelings into a tightly shut box, just to keep moving. You will piece together the puzzle that has been your life all along, finding connections that you never knew existed, until the magical moment when you are ready to accept the truth about all of us:

We have a beginning and an end.

There are no perfect answers. Our new friend, Grief, is a mixed bag of nuts. I have really learned to love her, but she is high maintenance to say the least. If I'm honest, though, I couldn't have lived this life without her. I need her. She teaches me. She makes me think. She reflects to me all the most important things. She's made me more compassionate. She helps me to help myself. She helps me help others. She has carried me through my darkest days, back into the light again.

Find a spot to settle in with us. Your two new friends, Greta and Grief. Wine? Water? Coffee? Diet Coke? Tea? Let's nestle in and talk a little. Jammies? Suits? Sweats? Blankies? I'm in for whatever works for you. I just want you to know that I'm here. Right beside you. Don't worry about Grief. If she gets blustery, I'll kick her under the table for you.

My biggest dream for this book is that she brings you comfort. She listens. Explains. Validates for you the very real experiences that you are having. She invites you to tell your stories. She reminds you that you don't have a deadline for wrapping up your grief or a quota for how many times you can release your feelings or words to convey your needs and desires moving forward from all that has been taken away from you.

Emote as if the spotlight belongs to you. Don't let anybody make you feel like there is something wrong with you because the feelings remain years or even decades later.

I hope this book assures and convinces you that there is no timeline. No alarm is about to ring, screaming, "Stop!" No sequence of events demands your loyalty for this ambiguous notion of "closure" to exist. First, denial. Second, anger. Third, bargaining. Fourth, depression. Fifth, acceptance.

Nope.

This book wants you to know you don't have to play by rule books that may or may not fit into your very real and unique acquaintance with Grief. You can throw the idea of "linear healing" into the tangled ball called your "real life." You can get lost in my stories that legitimize normal feelings.

The way you are coping right now won't be forever. You have

permission to accept that you are powerful enough to continue to regain a sense of normalcy and, yes—even great joy—as the seconds turn to minutes and minutes to days and days to weeks and weeks to months and months to years that follow your loss.

Come, dear reader, and rest your weary head.

Lean into my spirit.

Turn the page when you feel ready and just breathe.

REAL COUCHES

There are real couches
That you sit on
As you learn to create
Imaginary spaces
Able to hold you
In the same manner
That a pillow holds a head
When it falls upon
A bed to rest—
Ready at last
To release your countless
Thoughts and feelings
Stored for just the right moment

ASHLEY'S COUCH

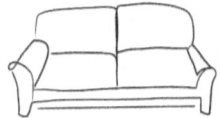

I'll never forget the first question that Ashley asked me as I nervously sat on my own hands, warming them on the weightless, down-filled couch that placed me dead-center, gazing into her sage-like eyes. *Tell me about your first memory with grief.*

It was as if we were playing a game of life-sized Jenga, and Ashley, in that one second in time, gently slid the weakest piece out as I watched the tower of my life crumble to the ground. I had with a steady hand been able to keep it standing for so long, but not today. Today was different. It was the first day of *real* healing for me. Healing that had been imprisoned for thirty-five years because I knew no other way to survive the magnitude of grief that I had harbored for so long. Pretending that it didn't exist was my only hope for survival. Spending my time supporting other people who were hurting was my specialty, and the perfect diversion from actually addressing my own loss that was secretly nudging me to wake up and feel.

The room where Ashley and I met was comforting. Simply decorated in soft blues and beige, cozy seating with soft pillows, one box of Kleenex, the sound of waves, lights dimmed. It was as if I were unzipping my mother's womb to crawl back in again. Ashley's celestial voice floated toward me like love on the wind while her eyes, clear and big like the ocean, danced like the ebb and flow of the warm water crashing into me. The intensity of my new therapist's stare was somewhat uncomfortable, while at the same time conveying her total commitment to lose herself inside of the words I decided to share. It was *my* story to tell today. The transcripts of my life had been stored in a vault, and today was the day I would place them at her feet, sweep away the dust, and begin to speak their name.

Years of compounded grief were begging for release; all about to be set free because my mother had finally passed away. It was as if that single event made way for a million other memories to be reborn. The contractions were so painful, but I knew the relief that would accompany their deliverance.

So far, all the boxes for my dream therapy session were checked, leaving me vulnerable for whatever it was that was about to happen to me. Ashley reminded me of the doctor who delivered my first child. There was something so serene about her. So gentle, yet confident. She was ready for a simple initial intake and exchange, while concurrently armed with a first aid kit should we turn in the direction of an emergency procedure.

I immediately sensed her competence and depth of knowledge without needing proof of advanced degrees or years of service. Having been an instructional mentor myself, I knew the tricks of coaching and the sensitive ground one must navigate when instilling trust in their mentee. Ashley's aura immediately put me at ease, pointing me in the directions of my self-chosen doors. She was prepared to lead, but more inclined to stay in her own lane and empower me to reroute my pain in a direction of healthy healing.

I strapped on my emotional seatbelt and literally began to projectile cry. At last the dam was breaking and my life was about to flood toward this stranger who would become the greatest gift I've ever known. Peering back in time, it was total confirmation that earth angels are, in fact, a real thing.

Where do I start? Which memory do I choose? Like a tsunami, my wheels began to spin with an uncontrollable force bearing down on me, replaying my memories like a movie in my head. Was my first memory with grief when a real person left this earth, or was it being pulled from my mother's arms to go into a nursery that I loathed as she tried to be a working mother? I *hated* everything about Little People Daycare. I wanted *her*!! All the time. How dare she try to abandon me with total strangers? And now, she had the audacity to die, leaving me forever this time, catapulting me into a pit of grief that included every other loss I had ever suppressed. It was if I had permission to finally face the pain that I had pushed aside over many years of dealing with *her* grief from a life so full of turmoil. (My mother had her share of pretty tough circumstances.) I had pushed and pushed and pushed the ball under the water, and the weakness of my arms could no longer withstand the pressure to keep it down under the surface.

My path to Ashley began one brave day with one fearless phone call. It was six months after my mother passed away, into the night and over the stars and through galaxies into her next life. Ashley was a hospice counselor, a life saver, a listener with ears that cried, "I hear you loud and clear!"

That courageous day I picked up the phone to call hospice, my palms dripped with sweat, commanding my nervous system to stand at attention. I remember it like it was yesterday because I am usually the giver. So awkward with accepting or getting help, but there I was. Paralyzed in my own grief. On my knees, pleading for help. Thank God for the clarity I felt that day as I pulled out my cell phone and dialed the number for the "Pink Team" that still rested in my contact list.

"I don't even know what to say to you," I started. "My mother passed away six months ago, and somebody told me that I was eligible for counseling for the next year through hospice."

The voice on the other side of the phone instantly comforted me, telling me that they knew "just" the person for me, and her name was Ashley. She *was* my perfect person, and that would come to light immediately following our first session.

I showed up early for our initial meeting, of course. I always show up early to appointments, building in extra time in case I get lost. Why is it that my sister holds an atlas of the universe in her head and navigates it perfectly like a human Google Map, while I? *I* could get lost driving home from work every day to the same house, on the same street, in the same neighborhood in which I have resided for a quarter of a century.

As I sat there trying to find the right words to share with Ashley, the memories of my mother's passing were as fresh as the lavender-scented candle burning on the table before me. Her question injected me into a time machine that couldn't decide where to take me. Too many starting points. My earliest memories of separation. The thoughts of how I ended up on this couch. My dad being crushed by early-onset Alzheimer's. My best friend from high school, gone at thirty-five after running a marathon. How can you drink too much water? The most obvious loss that I could identify prior to my mother and father dying—my brother's accident. But the real reason I thought I was there was because the loss I felt after my mother died was gripping me, strangling my flow, shutting me down.

For a moment inside of my head, I was back in time, two weeks before my beautiful mother died.

She gazed at me with those striking green eyes and professed, *I feel so sad for you.*

Why? I naturally replied.

Because you are going to miss me so much!

I can still hear the music playing in the background. My mother listened to a Kenny G CD on a continuous loop to soothe her mind that spun in that same ruminating circle for years. You could find no deeper thinker than she. How many times had I walked into her apartment to the sound of those crisp saxophone notes and the smell of a homemade meal like her sloppy joe's? Each time I wanted to gobble it up like I did as a child, but now that she was approaching eighty my fear for how long it might have been sitting on the counter held me back from tasting it. Each time I visited now, there were stacks of dishes to do, with flies circling their runways of delight. The food was prepared but never partaken. Ugh. More dishes for me to clean and food to discard.

Do all old people do that? Would I do that someday, too? She would go through the ritual of carefully measuring each ingredient to perfection. The house would warm up with the enticing smell of a meal that you couldn't find in a drive-through, evidence that the effort was so worth it with the first bite that melted in your mouth like butter sliding down a freshly warmed cinnamon roll, but she didn't want to eat. She preferred to sit hunched over her computer, digesting the latest news of the day, all of which she could recite to you in painstaking detail. This was the only nourishment she craved. The more days that passed, the less interest she had in adding anything to her body that wasn't essential for survival. Amazing, in the end, how few calories our bodies need to endure another day.

She required interaction with me much more than she needed or wanted food and water. I was her oxygen. She called me her oxytocin for the peace and healing that I induced when we were together. The real pandemic had not been Covid, she often stated. It was loneliness. I thanked God for the internet, where at least she could access another world to "think" alongside her in some parallel universe when I was not physically present.

How many women like me? How many? How many countless women are there frantically attempting to always be all places for all people? Like a zombie marching in and out of my own home, work, the grocery store, the pharmacy, the doctor, her apartment, I found myself wrapped in my own bandages that were cutting off my circulation, leading me only to a reflection of my own blank stare that had no idea which path to follow.

She had numerous notebooks beside her workspace with hundreds of quotes and briefs all prepared for the courtroom of life. She longed for conversation and gathered launching points for anybody willing to listen. Unlike my father who had been diagnosed with early-onset Alzheimer's in his late fifties, her brain continued to perform at a superior level to most, placing her in the highly gifted range. It exhausted me in a fun way. My intellect so uncapable of matching hers; however, there was that oxytocin thing I mentioned. My emotional intelligence bantered back and forth with her brain power, choreographing the perfect dance.

What is a mind without trust, emotion, love, regulation, connection to feed it? We needed each other. Together, there existed a feeling of completion that nobody else could provide. It was as if the umbilical cord that provided for my nourishment as a fetus was now regenerating, only this time it was I who was transferring well-needed nutrients to her in an eleventh-hour attempt to prolong her life.

I can still feel my fingers running across the tattered and torn fabric that comprised her sitting chair. The chair in which she sat across from my father for five decades, discussing all that mattered in the world. After my father passed away, she kept his glasses, wedding ring, and bible upon her side table for easy manipulation, not unlike worry beads. This chair is where I would find her each time I came to visit, perfectly sculpted into the shape of her body alone.

The smell of her lotion mixed with tobacco as the sound of oxygen hummed in and out of the tubing that adorned her small, princess-like facial features. Yes, she still snuck her cigarettes, despite the havoc they had wreaked in her life-giving lungs. Even the pangs of COPD could not fight the cravings that came from smoking since she was thirteen years old.

Her nightgown was worn so thin it looked like tissue paper, full of holes and strings hanging from the bottom, with her refusal to change into other outfits as the days continued to pass and bring her closer and closer to her last one. There were no baths or long showers at this point. The simple act of running a warm cloth across her translucent skin was refreshing enough.

For a moment, I slip back into reality, realizing that I am nestled against the pillow on Ashley's couch. The sound of waves and the dull lighting has lulled me into a trancelike state. It is only my first session, but the insight is already beginning to beckon me.

I realize I am here.

On this couch.

Not with my mother. I'm with Ashley.

I did it. I moved.

I took action toward figuring out what needed to happen for me to feel whole again.

Have you ever stopped to imagine if maybe completely and utterly falling apart could be a superpower instead of a weakness? Like my mother, I had worn unwavering strength like a badge of honor my whole life. *"We"* don't fall apart. *"We"* keep it together. *"We"* are always there to uplift others in pain, but don't need anything ourselves.

Are you kidding me?

Right here, right now, I was about to discover that I, too, deserved that same caring. After years of perfecting caregiving, I had missed the one and most important nugget.

If I didn't care for myself, too, I was going to be the one to die first.

For one more second, I stood at the edge of time. It seemed like the place that might exist between "right now" and "long ago." I felt like I was outside of my body looking down upon the two of us, still together in the same room as we laughed until we cried.

My mother was *so* right.

I was going to miss her beyond any worthy explanation. I was going to miss her so much that I would lose myself. Who was I without her?

If only I had known that she would be gone from this Earth a mere fourteen days later, I would have never left her. But I couldn't have known because that is not a privilege we have. No time-stamped, predetermined exit slips are delivered to prepare us for these moments. Our gift is only the ability to craft out time for the ones that we love, or to hone in on our abilities to be mindful and in the moment with our loved ones *right now*. Not that easy, is it?

There was work to do, bills to pay, kitchens to clean, groceries to purchase and transform into life-sustaining nourishment, relationships to cultivate, prescriptions to pick up, dogs to take out. I scrambled to figure it all out. To-do lists fell short, but still I made them with fifty-plus items, impossible to complete in a day, causing the pressure to only feel greater and more out of control.

Snap back, Greta. Ashley is waiting for an answer.

Wait.

What did Ashley ask me?

Did I answer it yet?

How long have I actually been sitting with her?

How much longer until some timer goes off and she asks me in her most polite manner to please leave so the next sad human can enter?

My mother had been sick for years. Decades, really, if you count the days that followed the death of my brother. The day he left, I felt as if she died, too. Or at least she wanted to, and I sat on the sidelines trying my best to cheer on "life" while she fought it tooth and nail all the way. She could never pull her feet back to the solid ground from before my brother's accident, and at times I literally hated her for that.

I didn't really hate her.

In fact, I loved her so much that I silently pleaded my case for her return every day and every night for the next thirty-five years.

Focus, Greta, I tell myself.

Tell me about your first memory with grief.

Just try and answer the question simply. Let Ashley lead the way.

Okay, Ashley.

"My brother died in a head-on collision with a semi-truck two weeks before I graduated from the University of Florida. He was ejected from the car, breaking almost every single bone in his body. I felt like my mother died that day, too. At least the mom I knew and loved every day up until that moment. Within a year, I broke up with the guy I thought I might marry. Correction: he broke up with me. I have never felt more alone in my entire life as I navigated the beginning of my adult life and career working with children with severe behavioral disorders, while my own mother drank herself to sleep every night to make herself forget that Tony was never coming home again."

Boom.

Childhood done. Here we go.

Fast forward. It feels like I was lost in a time warp for hours, then suddenly jerk back into reality—the present moment, where I realize where I really am. The timer softly murmurs inside of Ashley's loving hands. We both stare at each other with warm tears trickling like baby brooks down our cheeks.

"Well," she says. "If you feel comfortable with me, we can set up another appointment."

Comfortable? I think. *I feel more than comfortable.* It's as if I have known Ashley my whole life. Did she even respond to me at all during the last hour? I think maybe she uttered ten of the most perfectly chosen words I've ever heard, speaking volumes.

"I do," I state. *In fact, Ashley, I totally believe in synchronicity and timing, and up until this point I have never felt "ready." But this feels different.*

She leans into me and says, "I'm going to tell you something I've never told anybody before in a session. When I was in college, *my* brother was killed in a car accident. I feel it, too, Greta."

In that moment, I feel one of the highest frequencies of energy and love I have ever known—an affirmation from the universe that I was placed in this exact moment in time for a reason. My faith multiplies exponentially, and it becomes one of those signature moments in my life when I don't question the divine timing of our connection, I just feel gratitude.

I look over to my right and sitting beside me is my good friend, Grief. I can't help but thank her, for she guided me onto this couch and straight into the arms of my healer.

FOLLOW THEIR LEAD

Every night, I close my eyes and
Dreams take me places
Like empty passports begging to be stamped
With a million meant-to-be memories—
Moments that were meant to be lived with you,
But you're gone.
So, I can only meet you in my dreams.
Waiting for your presence...
I follow their lead
To the messages
That will awaken me.

YEAR OF DREAMS

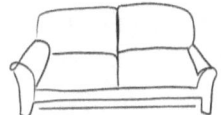

Do you think it's true that your heart only holds so many beats before you leave this Earth? The internet says that it is a myth. But I like to think that when your ticket is up, it is up. I wonder if we knew how many days we had left, how many heartbeats were remaining, would we live differently? Perhaps knowledge of this secret would grant us a fast-pass to greater fulfillment? Greater love and understanding of others? Deeper appreciation for all that we are and all that we have? Increased risk-taking for grand adventures? More wisdom and kindness to sprinkle on everything around us at a faster rate? Less sweat over the "small stuff"?

There Grief sat, whispering a million questions in my ear.

Visiting Ashley had me thinking all the time now. I have always been an overachiever, so why in the world would I not want to get an "A" in grieving too? I almost wanted Ashley to assign me a research project or something to give me a focus for the expansive reflection that was going on inside my head. My dad used to chuckle at this tendency of mine. He called it analysis to the point of paralysis. "Let the river flow by itself," he would say. Boy, I still love that visual. Me on a raft, floating in crystal-clear water. On my perfect day, the air is the slightest bit cool with the sunshine kissing my shoulders. I'm lying on my back, hands behind my head, staring up into an empty blue sky without a care in the world. Let's throw in some very soft bird chirping as well. No paddles or engines necessary. Why? Because the river knows the way.

The current of my river was rapid. Even after one session with Ashley, I was beginning to remember things. Things I didn't want to remember—but there she was, my partner in crime, Grief. She found glory in prodding me on to open up the book of my life and flip through the pages. Her confidence was admirable as her long finger pointed at the defining moments that had carried me through, from when I first learned that my brother was killed all the way to this instant nearly 35 years later.

I couldn't go anywhere without making connections in my head. Some made perfect sense. Some were just poetic expressions for a soul (mine) who was searching for the meaning in it all. I saw life's cycles everywhere I went now.

That Christmas, my youngest daughter had planted bulbs perfectly spaced alongside our driveway. Four out of six of them immediately burst their way out of the soil and toward the sun, but two didn't make it. At first, I thought that was a pretty good ratio. *They just weren't meant to blossom,* I thought. But then, to my surprise, about five weeks later, I came home and saw those two bulbs fighting like champions to emerge from the dirt. Who dare say they were not ready for full bloom? Protected, not buried, were they.

Everything reminded me of my grief. I was the late bloomer covered by a deeper layer of darkness. This darkness was not meant to preclude me from my rightful growth, but more to keep me safe until, at last, I was ready to rise up, even stronger than before. Most of us do not do things until we are "ready" to do them.

My mother always paraphrased a sentiment that my grandmother would repeat to her: "God protects fools and children, and you are both." Mama had gotten pregnant at sixteen with my brother—in my Nanny's eyes, definitely a foolish move. I, too, was vulnerable at the age of twenty-two when my brother died, so lacking in wisdom and understanding of loss. A fool and a child indeed. I needed somebody to watch over me, that's for sure, but I was also as strong as an ox (in my own mind) and ready to pull my "heavy" load all by my lonesome—or so I thought. My mother hopelessly wanted (maybe even needed) me to dive into the deep end of her pool of tears with her, but I couldn't. I didn't have the wherewithal to stay above the water for air. I would have drowned, so I treaded on the surface of feeling anything.

Frankly, I numbed out. I desperately needed to believe that life was worth living. That it was the beginning of my life, not the end. So, I did what any other wise young woman might do: I threw myself into a million other activities to distract myself from the real pain.

And that's okay. The pain was willing to wait for a lifetime to be confronted.

I threw myself straight into 12-to-14-hour workdays, earning me the Rookie Teacher of the Year Award. There were nights I stayed at school until 10 p.m. creating more plans, more activities, more distractions, all in the name of children. Or was it really my defense mechanism? It was something I could control. Something that could fill space in my head that might otherwise be filled with pain for my mother.

You see, at this point, me feeling my own pain didn't appear to be an option. My perception was that it was all about my mother's pain—and folks, your perception is your reality.

I witnessed the intense pain my parents were experiencing, and I wanted to take it away from them. I wanted nothing more than their happiness. In fact, I *needed* it, because it was in direct correlation to my happiness. I also couldn't fathom my parents experiencing any more heartache or worry. So what did I do? I became Little Miss Everything. I became the ultimate "solo performer." I refused to allow myself to trust or need anyone—therefore, eliminating any chance of further pain or disappointment. Keeping myself "safe."

It would take me years to realize this was a trauma response, rushing in to hold my aching heart.

Because of this, my thoughts related to the deep loss I had experienced began to go lower into the recesses of my mind. My dream zone was rich with material and my subconscious mind was more than pleased to write a manuscript. That's when the year of dreams began.

I had never experienced panic attacks before, but now for some reason the cars around me seemed to be driving faster and more aggressively. I didn't have "official" panic attacks, but semi-trucks felt like Empire State Buildings closing in all around me, stealing my air. The air I needed to breathe. The sound of an ambulance was a trigger, for it was the same sound others must have heard when they witnessed my brother's accident. The one that threw him from his car like a shooting star never to be seen again. *Slow down your breathing*, I thought. Instinctually, I knew there must be some connection between the rate of my heartbeat and the speed at which my brain was processing my newfound fear of death.

I had forgotten the details until I saw Ashley. Forgotten about the year of dreams that followed my brother's passing for 365 days in a row. I kid you not: each night as I slipped away into my deep slumber, my brother appeared to me. The theme was the same, but the venue was different. Each night I ran into my brother and our conversation flowed something like this:

Oh, my God, Tony!! You're alive! You'll never believe this. Mom thought you were dead. You have to come with me. She'll be so excited!

In my dreams, it always felt as if Tony and I were walking toward my mother, but we never arrived. I still had the "good" feeling that I was about to give my mother the greatest gift she could ever have—my brother back. Alive.

Each night, I could feel the excitement of finding him, knowing that I was about to fix every problem my mother was facing—the pain, the loss, the transformation of her identity. After all, who was she if she wasn't the sixteen-year-old girl who had given birth to a beautiful baby boy named Tony? Her life couldn't have been a mistake if *he* was the result.

One night I dreamed Tony was in the grocery store, stocking up on crisp green onions, aromatic cloves of garlic, tender pork, ginger, and salty soy sauce. His favorite foods were rich in scent, flavor, and culture. Mom would spend hours mixing her magic to please his palate with his beloved Chinese cuisine.

The next night, I would see him at the movies, handing his ticket over for entry. I found him each night at sporting events, bookstores, live theatre performances, school campuses, and more. Each time, my words were the same.

Oh, my God, Tony!! You're alive! You'll never believe this. Mom thought you were dead. You have to come with me. She'll be so excited!

Walk with me. Let's go find her and fix her life. Let's make everything normal again. Side by side, we would begin the stroll toward her, but we never reached her before I woke up.

And then the final night came.

Tony was full-garb pilot. He looked like the male version of Amelia Earhart. Leather cap, jacket, scarf, goggles. The dream started the same way as it always did.

Oh, my God, Tony!! You're alive! You'll never believe this. Mom thought you were dead. You have to come with me. She'll be so excited!

I should mention here that each night up until this moment, Tony was always as happy to see me as I was to see him. But on this night, he began to pull away from me.

Leave me alone. I'm fine! I'm not coming with you. I'm okay. You need to leave me alone. Let me go.

What?? Tony disappeared into the night. Without me. Walking away from me. No desire to stay. I was left devastated and alone. *What will I do now? He doesn't want to be with me anymore. How will I ever make things right for Mom if he is unwilling to come with me?*

My heart was racing, tears rolling down my cheeks, staring into space as my body popped up from a deep dream state. Tony was ready for flight in a new direction.

Somehow, I managed to fall asleep for a couple of hours after waking. The next day, I headed immediately to the guidance counselor's office at my school to seek advice.

Her name was Linda. She was a wise and gentle woman. If not for women like her, I never would have survived my first year in a very difficult teaching situation. She generously passed on what she knew to me, accelerating my learning with great care.

That day, she moved her chair closer so she could grab my hands in hers. After the loss of my brother (and what felt like losing my mother, too), I was drawn to strong, maternal women. I snuggled close to them like a cell phone recharging its battery. She listened to my words, which is how she always started. Watching her absorb other people's thoughts and feelings to ensure that she had all the "just right" information to move forward never ceased to amaze me. I loved watching her share her gift with children, and this day I was the one receiving it. Grief's child.

I cried as I shared my year of dreams with her. I had never told anybody about it. My own analysis left me lost and confused about why Tony would no longer want to be part of our family. I had lost hope for finding answers to comfort my mother. I was afraid about the impact of Tony's missing chair at our family table, the loss of his contributions to our joy, and the fact that my mother might never be the same woman I worshipped before his accident. I had no idea about where my life was headed. Sometimes, I wished that it had been me who died so I didn't feel so much responsibility for life. I felt unrest. Mixed emotions. Pressure to perform at a level that would never disappoint. I was living for both of us now. Every unrealized dream of Tony's rested upon my shoulders. My arms felt weary as I raised the bar in countless attempts to erase my mother's agony and comfort her with fleeting seconds of happiness.

But Linda gave it the insight I needed to hear.

"Did it ever occur to you that your brother is telling you he is at peace? Maybe he doesn't need to come back with you, because he is good?"

What?? What did she just say? You mean this crazy year of dreams might have just led me to another one of my starting points? (Can you have multiple points of origin for growth? I think you can.)

I left her office, beginning to wonder. Maybe, there is something so beautiful after we die that the person who leaves us resides in total peace. I began to trust the beauty of something magical and mystical in the afterlife that we can't "see" but we can feel. Like the bulb waiting to rise from the dark because it needed time to prepare, I cracked through the soil of my own dirt ceiling. I would come to believe that death is not a final bow, but more a transition into the next phase of eternal life surrounded by great love and light.

I never had that dream about Tony again. But, in my waking life, I began to dream of days where Tony's death wasn't the only thing my family would think about, and I pondered other ways to support my mother's healing that didn't involve me completely losing myself in her pain. There would come a day when I would only sit in *my* loss, free of the self-imposed pressure demanding me to comfort my mother first.

I began to take notes, some written, some in my head. *Note to self: tell Ashley about the year of dreams.*

FINAL CALL

Landing on her feet every time
She pranced like a cat
Overly confident
With the number of lives she had left
Unafraid to risk it all
Because she knew
The final call was still
Four lives away

NINE LIVES

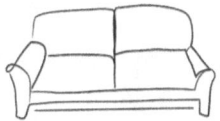

Ashley listened in a way I had never witnessed before. Listening has always been a struggle for me. I swear, it is not because I don't think what you have to say is important. It's just that I get so excited to be a part of rich conversations. My mind is filled with questions I want to ask and insights I want to share.

Ashley was special, though. She could sit in silence. That was something I could never do.

No matter what situation I was in, when the silence became too loud, I would jump in to fill the space with something that seemed valuable. I'm still learning to sit in silence. To be open to the messages that float on air without being spoken. To accept invitations to process words and turn them into meaning without the vocal collaboration of others. We have two ears and one mouth for a reason.

The sessions with hospice counseling continued, and I found myself obsessed with wanting to narrate my mother's life. I needed every breath that she had taken to stand for something. I was her voice now. I was a human oxygen tank that would keep her alive for all eternity. I was the legacy that would stand tall proclaiming, *You mattered!*

And you still matter.
And you will always matter.
And you are matter.

You never left me. You just represent changes in property: texture, shape, and state. I feel you, and I know with all my heart that you remain.

My favorite days continue to be the ones when unexpected goosebumps cover my arms, my hair standing up straight. I gently run my hands down my own arms to feel my skin acknowledging that my angels are present. It's a "different" kind of goosebump feeling than what you might be thinking about. Trust me, you know when this kind happens because it gives you a rush of oxytocin and you sense an energy force surrounding you with bright light. The two main ingredients for angels.

Beginning therapy opened up a thunderous roll of disconnected thoughts and feelings inside me. I trusted it would all be meshed together by my mind, so desperately searching for clarity and comfort. I believed that it would be sewn together like a beautiful quilt I could hang on my wall of remembrance. The webs branched out in the following manner.

My mother was born at home in a bedpan. Can you imagine that? Her mother, my Nanny, had a stillborn, too. I had a miscarriage before my oldest daughter, and both of my pregnancies involved emergency procedures to save my life because my placenta grew into my uterus, so I wonder sometimes what might have happened if I had given birth at home like my grandmother.

Do you ever stop to ponder if your entry into this world impacts you later in life? I was born in a blizzard. My sister was only two-and-a-half pounds when she was born prematurely, and the doctors told my mom that she had died because they didn't think she would make it. How insane that they thought telling her this would prepare her for a loss that never even occurred.

My mother's childhood reminded me a lot of Fern from

Charlotte's Web by E.B. White. She grew up on a farm and begged her dad to save the runts. We still have the picture of my petite pony-tailed mom holding her piglet named Snooty with a baby bottle nestled between her chest and his mouth. My mom was a natural mother in many ways, but I doubt "little Fern" knew she would become pregnant at the age of sixteen.

By the time she was thirty-three years old, my brother was sixteen. Such a contradiction to my own life, waiting until I was thirty-three to get married and thirty-five to have my first child. I often gaze at my own twenty-three-year-old daughter imagining two small children by her side, aged five and three. It seems implausible.

I can promise you that my mother becoming a teenage parent absolutely impacted my upbringing. In some ways, it was like a birthday party every day. My parents put a youthful spin on every event (holidays, birthdays, game days, church days, Fridays, etc.), and all our friends were drawn to the excitement they unveiled. My parents would sit for hours in conversation with us, always seeming to "understand" in a way that other parents did not, and most definitely accepted the variations in our development. My passion for inclusion, diversity, and seeking to understand others grew daily through my observation of their loving encounters with our peer group.

Of course, the funny side to this story is that my mother implanted the fear of God in me regarding premature sex. That is how I ended up with her infamous "shiny penny" letter my junior year in high school.

Sex is like fire, she wrote. *It can be incredibly warm and protective. But just like fire, it can be extremely destructive.*

She went on to share:

Dare to be so rare that only someone who values and respects that power might be lucky enough to have you.

Now, here's where the "shiny penny" part comes in. She actually taped a brand-new, shiny penny to the bottom of the letter.

After this beautiful depiction of my fire being the prize for the guy who truly understands, respects, and earns my warmth, she wrote: *A brand-new penny loses it shine after being in too many pockets!*

Yup. That was Mom. She had a way of sneaking a huge lesson on promiscuity into the mix of safe, intimate, and meaningful sex. The lessons of her own life often became my classroom.

She grew up in a small town. Her mother was what we might refer to now as "a bad-ass." My grandmother wore pants, and she was good at math. She was the best storyteller I ever knew. She would scoot up on her chair and touch your face and your body while she captivated you with a performance rather than a mere "read aloud"—like interactive theatre. A graduate from Purdue, she helped my grandfather run a granary business—she did the books. Because of this, another woman had to care for my mother all day. Mom called her "Ms. Ederds" as it rolled off her tiny tongue easier than "Edwards." She loved Ms. Ederds so much that she thought she was her real mother until about the age of three.

I believe that is one reason my mom took the role of mother so seriously. It was her full-time job and devotion. Her mother had been absent in some ways, so she never wanted us to question that she was the mama bear. Her identity was tightly wrapped around the presentation of our home, our education, and our futures. She stood erectly next to my father at work functions, dressed impeccably for the role of supportive wife, often being the brains behind his success.

Her father, Vernon, was a kind man. She told stories of his silent philanthropic gestures to help people in need throughout the town. No doubt this ingredient was mixed into our family "soup." I am most thankful that I came from loving stock, and my desire to help others and find ways to grow love in this world holds my body up in the same manner in which your bones do. Guess I got some of that from 'ole Vernon. A portrait of him hung in our home, a plump cigar dangling from the corner of his mouth. That's how he died.

"Esophageal cancer," Mom explained, "because he always had that cigar dripping down his throat."

Sadly, Vern died when my mother was only nineteen. The pain she endured was so overwhelming, and now she held two babies in her arms and was imprisoned in an abusive relationship. Nothing was good enough for her first husband. "Cold" food and ironed clothes with one miniscule wrinkle came crashing down on the floor to remind her of her weakness.

Such a polar opposite to the silent, serving father who had raised her. She told me several times that she was unable to attend his funeral—and by "unable," I mean emotionally ill-equipped. I never understood how my mother could miss her own father's service. I never understood, that is, until I found myself incapable of planning a service for her. There was Grief again, giving me lessons on empathy and understanding. Pointing that long finger to the moment in my book of life that I would feel remorse for the judgment I had cast upon my teenage mother standing in the depths of grief, holding her two babies under the age of three, trying to escape a toxic marriage. My God, the intensity of loss she must have felt.

When my mother died, I tried. I tried repeatedly to write eulogies, to choose venues, to plan menus for a celebration of life, to write programs, to orchestrate just the right music... but in the end, I simply could not do it.

I was frozen in my own loss, while also obsessed with the thought that nothing would be good enough to convey the darkness of my life without her. There was no light at this point for me. No festivity that would allow me the grace to celebrate her life. Not yet.

While Grief continued to lightly urge me in the right direction, she also waited patiently for me to discover the appropriate time for me to honor my mother's life. She had countless discussions affirming my choices. She knew, just as I did, that my love for my mother was never in question. She knew that if anybody, indeed, understood my inability to move forward, it would have been my mother. Grief held me for months, encouraging the unfolding of my story, until at last it would become a book dedicated to my mother. The greatest gift I could give a woman whose love language centered around acts of service and affirmation was the first book that I authored. I dedicated it to her and launched it on the third anniversary of her passing.

My mother was raised with all the social graces. When we ate soup, she said things like, "Little ships go out to sea, push my spoon away from me." Burping was forbidden. Handwritten thank you cards were mandatory. Antiques graced our home and she explained that we never "owned" them; rather, we were the safekeepers of them for the next generation. The marble-topped washstand was a monument for one of my great-great-grandmothers who had crossed the United States in a covered wagon, demanding the only way she would move was if that washstand came with her, and so it did.

My mother danced for years, and people noticed the graceful manner with which she pointed her toes as she drifted across the room like a ballerina even in her last years. She stood in third position without trying. It was the natural opening move for her delicate, dainty body to glide toward others.

My Nanny had fancy furniture and big St. Bernards that they would sit me upon when I was a baby, as if I was riding a horse. We have thousands of pictures to prove these things, and I sifted through them regularly to mentally recite our family memories, as my mother also placed great importance upon the true and sacred art of storytelling and the preservation of your oral history.

My mom had nine lives.

There were so many times that it would have made sense for her to die. Sessions with Ashley reminded me of that, and Grief sat alongside me as if we were creating a timeline of my mother's near-misses. "Ah, yes. I remember that time," she would say, as I relived the moments my dear mother barely hung on to her own breath. She survived multiple cancers and surgeries that left her frail body aching, like when surgeons had to remove part of her ribcage to take her diseased kidney, or when complications during a routine hip surgery left her in the intensive care unit for weeks, or when she simply tried to lift a heavy pail and broke vertebrae in her back, her brittle bones snapping from severe osteoporosis.

The pictures in my mind had to be addressed, and Ashley knew that. It was the only way in which I would be able to create new pictures.

Little ships go out to sea, push my grief away from me.

Open the antique washstand drawer. Take out the picture of Mom and Snooty the runt. Run your fingers across the antique recipe box that belonged to Nanny. Make soup to soothe your tears.

My mother was far from perfect—but as close to perfect as possible at the same time. As each year passed, I began to realize my own imperfections and forgive myself for the times I had secretly judged her for doing the best she knew how at the time. Oh, the wisdom that comes with maturity.

She was a survivor. As a young woman, I found myself so confused about the juxtaposition of her Herculean strength and the fragility of her outer shell. I saw the rapidity with which she cracked but overlooked her capacity to become stronger with each blow—more capable of protecting herself from future injury, dodging punches like a seasoned boxer.

She kept walking, one foot in front of the other, through the night that her first husband held her captive at the kitchen table with a gun held to his chest. Through the first night in this world without her son Tony. Through the night I corralled my roaming father with Alzheimer's back to our sides as I watched over her in the emergency room after she swallowed over 200 pills because she just didn't think she could handle the loss of his once-brilliant mind.

The hardest moment of my entire life, I think, was the feeling of my mother's body slipping away from me the day she died. I had been more than her daughter for years. I was her caretaker. Her nurse. Her social worker. Her personal shopper. Her hospice liaison. Her maid. Her chef. Her physical therapist. Her driver. Her best friend and confidant. I knew exactly what she needed and how to deliver it—but not that afternoon.

Every other visit, it always started the same. I would enter her apartment, and if she was sleeping (which she did all the time toward the end of her life), I would go through the ritual of safely raising her from the bed. First, she would sit up to ground herself. Body up, glasses on, robe over shoulders. Second came toe wiggling. Shoes positioned strategically for easy entry directly below her bed, exactly in the spot that her walking feet would fall. Right foot preceding the left. Cough a few times to clear her lungs. Oxygen a must for transport. Teeth in. Now, move. Slow and steady wins the race.

It was a dance we had both perfected. We moved in tandem together, beautifully executing her awakening.

But this day... this day was *different*.

Like the cat who had always landed on her feet, I had expected this day to just be another example of her ability to persevere despite the evidence that she was actively dying. She had been sleeping for seventeen-plus hours a day. Her mental clarity had diminished. When I tried to explain for the hundredth time how to turn on the television with the remote control, she would stare at me like she had never heard it before. I drew diagrams and pictures for visual cues, but none of it stuck. Keep in mind, this was a woman who had a photographic memory. She was brilliant, but now she had been reduced to the frailest version of herself, left wondering why the world couldn't go back to the simplicity of a black-and-white TV with an "on" and "off" button.

My mother was the biggest creature of routine that you ever knew. The last thing her fingers touched every single night was the Kenny G CD that swayed her to sleep. I still can't listen to it without sobbing because I know that each note continues to play for her, wherever she rests.

That day, my oldest daughter was with my mother, and she called to tell me that Mom was requesting morphine. *What?* This woman, who had lived eight of her nine lives, was consenting to death? More—*inviting* it? My heart was racing faster than the engine of a racecar fighting to win the last leg of NASCAR. I needed to hurry up and do something to save her.

I rushed to her house and went straight to her bedside.

Let's go, Mom.

Ground yourself.

Your robe, glasses, shoes, teeth are all in position. I'm here to make sure you've got this.

I tried.

With all my might.

She only weighed sixty-seven pounds.

Unlike the million times before, on this day when she sat up, she began slipping out of my hands toward the floor. Tears came flooding out of my eyes, forecasting unbearable heartache. It was a different force of nature from what I had ever known prior. I could barely lift her back into the bed for safekeeping as I simultaneously grabbed the phone to speed-dial the "Pink Team."

The nurse answered as I pleaded for assistance. *I need you to come.*

Come now.

I don't know what to do.

She is slipping.

I can't hold her. This feels different. She wants morphine.

Nooooooo.

*I CAN **NOT** DO THIS ALONE.*

Have you ever seen a mercury thermometer break? We had one when I was little that somehow or another made it all the way into my adult home. My mother had always scared me to death that if you touch the mercury, you will die. Well, the day came when it fell from my fingers, crashing into a million pieces of shattered glass, and there rolled the magical, somewhat enticing ball of glimmering fright toward me. It reminded me of the color of the silver cot that my mother laid on after attempting to take her own life.

How potent would the force be on this day? It was rushing toward me, and I was horrified to pick it up, knowing at the same time that I could not let it sit there for fear of someone else being exposed to its powers. How could I continue to protect my mother, myself, and my family? It was *my* fear spinning now. Fear of finality. Fear of everything cracking open in a direction for which I was unprepared. Fear of cushioning others from the potential poison that begins the second morphine enters the mouth of your dying loved one.

You cannot turn back the actions meant to provide instant relief for the worn-down patient while simultaneously activating the greatest pain of the "providers" about to feel an emotional torture they've never known. In order to relieve my mother, I must accept that I would have to willingly harbor the future grief of our family and friends within the palm of my own hand that controlled the syringe.

Her nine lives began to flash before my eyes like some fabricated reel on Instagram.

One: Born in a bedpan.

Two: Sixteen years old and pregnant.

Three: Escape abusive husband without being shot.

Four: First-born child dies in a car accident.

Five: Thyroid and kidney cancer.

Six: Caretaker for husband with Alzheimer's.

Seven: Living through a suicide attempt.

Eight: Broken hip. Complications with surgery. ICU.

How was she still standing at all?

Nine: Morphine dosage number one of three.

Grief stood there, just staring at me. Neutral. That's the part of her that sometimes made me the angriest.

"I've been trying to tell you," she stated matter-of-factly. "You haven't been listening.

"Your mother is really dying this time."

CLUB INITIATION

The more you're "in,"
The more comfortable you become
Within your own skin.
It takes a while—
But you'll see what I mean
You think you want to leave, but then
a bolt
Becomes a lean.
You slowly allow yourself to
Listen and learn as you
Sway with the crowd of
Grievers
And angel believers
Who frequent the club.

SEE YOU AT THE CLUB

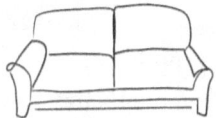

The death club is not necessarily on your bucket list, but it can be rather cool. Invite only, you know, so there's that. I was invited for the first time by my best friend, Hilary, at the age of fourteen.

I thought I was on the real VIP list when she poured out her story about how her mother had passed away. She shared copious journals with me, so I knew all there was to know about death at the beginning of my tenth-grade year in high school—right?

We shared tears together as I empathized with her loss. *What would life without your birth mother really feel like?* I wondered.

Being with Hilary always felt "extra." Her life was meant to be more than just average, and it showed in everything she said and did. Here she was barely in her teenage years, already teaching me about monumental things like her mother's eternal rest.

Our club meetings took place in her bedroom. We'd rush home from school, eat a snack, and slip into the corner of their house filled with her poetry and books, all tucked away with her deepest and most lovely feelings.

We felt like grown-ups and philosophers as we lost ourselves in her words meant to revive her mother if only for a moment or two. She tenderly handed memories of her mama to me like a prized gift, and I gladly accepted the treasure. I felt blessed to know her if only through the heartfelt expression of Hil's writing. We flipped through photographs of her mother revealing the almost identical features and personality traits they shared. I believed in those magical moments that I knew her, too, and I grew to understand what made my friend so exceptional.

I knew that even though her mother's life had been shortened, it had extreme and unending value. I knew that losing her so early gave my friend wisdom that other girls her age were incapable of grasping. I understood that she somehow lived on through her daughter.

She had given me a best friend and the world a great thinker and feeler who would continue to impact others for years to come in great ways. Her life stood for something, and it always would.

As the years passed, club meetings would take place in many different venues. Strict guidelines for location were non-existent, and club meetings could be called on-the-spot if needed, but the basics for club mentality were as follows:

Number one: the truth is, you've always been preparing for the club. You just didn't know it. Your life has been a series of gains and losses taking place from the second you were born.

The "playlist" of your life runs as you enter the room. All the songs that invoke great meaning and emotion for you from your early childhood upward spin on a continuous loop. Photo collages of your existence are hung on the walls as Carol King and James Taylor music serenades you into a mild melancholy (feel free to enter the music of your generation here).

The first few minutes you arrive, you have tiny pools of tears in your eyes and a warm feeling in your heart because you are learning about empathy and compassion for your friends who have been inducted into the Board of Directors of Grief before you.

As the first few years pass, you earn badges of strength for things like your dog passing away. Moving to another state. Your grandma dying. You handle all of that like a champion. (Just like Girl Scouts, you stitch patches to your belt with your varying levels of loss and acceptance.)

You have begun to pay for your membership in small installments, but your "lifetime" status arrives when you experience your most crushing loss—the grief that only you can describe. Nobody else gets to determine the magnitude of whatever it is that feels devastating to you. You, alone, are the author of that story.

To enter the clubhouse, you can scream as loudly as you want or gently tap on the door. You'll need to visit more frequently in the first year following a loss.

The "firsts" without them can be treacherous.

First birthday.

First Thanksgiving.

First Christmas.

Then it changes a bit, and grief surprises you at different unexpected corners, like that song that reminds you of standing in the kitchen with your mother dancing and cooking before your first child was about to be born.

Or seventeen years later, when that same baby is about to graduate from high school, but now you remember curling up next to your mother in bed as she silently slips into her next life. Only the two of you lying there together; you caress the arms that held you and that baby countless times.

You'll find yourself at the club door when you come across a photo of your father's hands holding your newborn baby, or when you hear the sound of his voice moving through your own vocal cords sharing a belief or a family mantra.

Once you're in the club, you will find ways to support the newest members. We are drawn to each other because our level of understanding has deepened, having experienced great loss firsthand.

I apologize in advance, but when I attend your family funerals, I cry harder than your loved ones do, because it is a total release of the grief that I don't express for my own family. Funny how that works. I have actually sobbed so heavily that others are shocked by my "relationship" with the deceased, who many times I barely even knew. It's my way of showing you I care, while also releasing my own trapped grief.

Grief attends all meetings but she alternates her level of involvement. The more I get to know her, the more I would describe her as an extroverted introvert. The last time I met her at the club, she brazenly came up to me like she had been drinking too much and was in charge of my intervention. You know—meant to call my attention to life matters that need addressing.

"Are you still hanging on to some unresolved grief?" she prodded. "Has ignoring it all these years helped you, or has it had an everlasting impact on your big life decisions—marriage, parenting, friendships, career, ability to take risks?"

She kept nudging to the point that I wanted to run away from the discomfort accompanying her line of questioning, but instead I listened with tears in my eyes.

The truth hurts sometimes, but it also sets you free.

I went to leave the club that night and as I turned to look back one more time, Grief was sitting at the bar. It was the first time that I saw her looking sad herself. It was if she realized for the first time that not everybody would be able to figure her out. Not everybody would accept her invitation to join the club readily.

I left feeling differently. Kind of like I needed to be her friend. Maybe if I could learn to like her, other people could too. Or at the very least, we could try. It wasn't her fault that she made people sad. She was just doing her job. She picked up a shot glass, slammed it back, and sauntered toward the exit. We both headed back to reality, knowing fully well that it wouldn't be the last time we would run into each other.

"See you at the club," she said.

I nodded and kept walking.

CONFINED

All the stars in the sky
Couldn't make
One more tear
Fall from my eyes.

ONE AND DONE

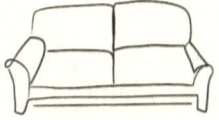

After my brother died, I felt like I didn't cry for the next ten years. Oh, I desperately *wanted* to cry, but the tears just wouldn't come. Immediately following a park-side memorial service for him—where we gathered to sing Beethoven's *Ode to Joy* and make references to Tony being with the stars and calling upon Antoine de Saint- Exupery to share his words of wisdom, reminding us that "it is only with the heart that one can see rightly; what is essential is invisible to the eye"—I began the journey to "move on."

Grief tried to stifle her giggles erupting as a result of my misguided conception that after a ceremonious acknowledgement of his life that supposedly we were "celebrating," I would be "done" and "okay." Instead, Grief snatched my salty tears, pouring them into a tightly sealed bottle that she hid in her pocket. She always watched me to determine my weakest moments, when she could release *just enough* pain to remind me of my high honor in the Grief Club—but not enough to cry.

I purposefully watched sad movies in hopes of sobbing uncontrollably. My entire body craved the shaking that might come like the backdraft of a fire. Well-sealed emotions so lacking in oxygen were confined in my body, begging for rapid explosion to help me release the pain of losing my brother and my mother, losing my hope, and losing my fearless life, all in the same instant.

That was what my life felt like—full of combustion. It was burning to the ground, and I had no way to stop the draft of air feeding its destruction. My mother wanting nothing more than to die caused me unbearable grief, and denying its existence was a must for survival. I was a brand-new teacher at the front end of new growth. Learning about life, adulting, and a career that needed me desperately to be fully present. While I was a teacher, in the School of Life I was the student that year, barely keeping up with the volumes of hands-on learning appearing like a mudslide in my "year of firsts" after Tony left. He left me when I needed him most to be the big brother, explaining to me what the hell was going on.

The first year after Tony passed away felt dreamlike. I floated above my own body, watching my life in zombie-like fashion, moving in and out of each day without noticing the pages of a calendar falling toward the year mark.

The day Tony died, my parents were told not to go to the hospital.

Trust us, they said.

You don't want to have this image in your mind for the rest of your life. Remember the good stuff.

Looking back, there was no "good stuff" that year. We couldn't handle it. Nothing seemed right without him, so instead we ignored the holidays, celebrations, events, and activities that might remotely remind us of the empty space left behind after his accident.

No Christmas.

No birthdays.

No laughter allowed for the next year.

In and out of every day, we drug our bodies toward darker corners, like emotional corpses purging our lives of all happiness with an insatiable hunger for self-destruction.

My mother ended up in the psych ward for a week. God, was

she mad at my father. Sitting in white robes with therapists guiding her to visualize balloons of sadness floating up into the sky to take her worries away. She was way too smart for that. She knew she could float away *with* them, still attached to the string that was strangling her. If it was up to her, she would have sailed farther and farther into the heavens toward my brother without looking back once to see if the rest of us were watching.

My father was just doing the best he could at the time. He saw her slipping away into a deep depression, drinking herself into oblivion. She needed to disappear to forget the nightmare that she was living. I needed emotional anesthesia to forget that my life seemed meaningless compared to Tony's death, which became the focal point of each breath we continued to take. I wanted to beg her to live for me. *Please. Just for today can we pretend that he didn't die?*

I read once the epitaph by Malloy: "When all that's left of me is love, give me away." The image that immediately arose in my mind was my mother and me invisibly connected by a string, comprised of love. I am standing on Earth while she gently floats away into the sky, over the rainbows, and into another place called Heaven.

Looking back over that first year after my brother passed, I can honestly say I have never felt another pain that compares. If you're wondering why, it's because I adapted quickly to the feeling of immense suffering by immediately laying the cement and bricks that would construct my great wall of protection.

First, I would need a trench for the foundation. Here I laid all the unwanted feelings, fears, and regrets surrounding the sudden death of my sibling. As I began to lay the brick and mortar, each layer permanently housed a unique "issue" that arises with the untimely death of a child.

One layer belonged solely to my parents experiencing this "out of order" loss.

One layer for my sister, who had been like Tony's twin growing up in trauma (from my mother's abusive first marriage) when they were only infants, creating a bond between them that was unbreakable.

Another layer for me, the baby and attention-seeker of the family, so used to laughing and deflecting pain off our family with great success.

Another layer for the loss of other relationships—namely, my emotionally vacant boyfriend at the time. He couldn't handle the intensity of the aftermath, so he left me once again standing all alone. Or truth be told, maybe it was me devoid of emotion? He had needs, too, right? *Oh, just put up the wall and block it out.*

Okay, this loss thing will be fine now that this strong, sturdy wall is standing. Nice. This should keep any other human from ever entering my love bubble. I would like to proclaim from this day forward that I will never allow myself to love anyone to the point of being hurt in the least if they should choose to go away. ("Go away" includes death). One and done!

Thank God my amazing husband would come along with arms the size of monster trucks to knock that wall down, pulling me from the wreckage.

For years I sat by phones and doors. Just waiting for bad news that I had lost somebody. I never left my sister's side, nor did she mine, as if we were each other's protectors. When my daughters first began driving, I stood by the door until they arrived home, a sick feeling in the pit of my stomach. *Please bring them back to me,* I prayed to God. I gave them ornaments of angels to hang in their cars and urged them to pray and wrap themselves in protective bubbles of love before they drove anywhere.

How must my mother have *really* felt after having a sheriff knock on the front door to share that Tony would never be driving home again? She told me she knew in the deepest part of her bones that something terrible had happened that day when his work called to inquire where he was because he was late. *He is never late for anything,* she thought.

So many lost moments consumed me, taking me away from the present moment. I could have never predicted that it would take more than three decades to truly confront my grief. Thirty plus years. My God.

Grief patted me on the back and winked. "Nobody told you this would be easy."

Note to self: ask Ashley how to stay present in the moment.

CAMOUFLAGED

Slowly over eggshells
Her toes on point danced between land mines
Designed to destroy her feeling heart.
In their ignorance some had called her an empath
For her highly attuned emotional grasp.
Little did they know she was always ready for
*   combat.*
Camouflaged in her protective smile.
She just wanted someone to hurl the grenade that
Would crack open the safe to reveal her own needs.
She needed a caretaker too.
It was her turn to be held.

CARETAKER

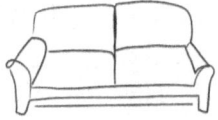

If you could choose only one word to describe your life, what would it be? Mine would probably be "caretaker." I knew the role better than any other, as it infused itself into all of my nooks and crannies. Even as a small child, I could be found in my room caring for twenty or more dolls on a daily basis. They each had a name and a distinct personality. I would teach them, read to them, bathe them, and rock them to sleep, tucking each one into the covers once night fell. Raggedy Ann was the one I favored. She had been a Christmas gift when I was about three years old. She was one of the oversized models, so when I received her she was actually as big as me. I felt so guilty that I got the real bed every night that sometimes I would choose to sleep on the floor so she could lay upon my mattress.

From the instant my brother died, I pulled from my expertise as a caregiver providing services for others in need. It comforted me to comfort others. It would become one of the biggest learning points of my lifetime. The leading question being: how do I care for myself at the same time as I care for others?

Why did this seem so difficult?

The deeper I went into my self-study with Ashley, the more I delved into this notion of myself as a person responsible for others. It all seems so ridiculous to me now—the extent to which I lost myself —but I was doing the best that I could at the time. There had definitely been traits of co-dependency strewn throughout our family history that snuck into my make-up. I was such a contradiction of independence and reliance upon what I offered to my family dynamics. I knew I brought great happiness to my parents, but occasionally it felt like a job. When I was in high school and college, they knew I would get good grades. They knew I would choose my peer group well. They knew I would pull my weight in extracurricular activities and participate in family functions. My people-pleasing powers were most likely a response to trauma that lie dormant in our early childhood. I didn't realize the manner in which my mother's life experiences infiltrated my actions, both in good and unhealthy ways. This self-imposed notion that I needed to man the helm of helpers stood in a solid foundation of cement. In every way that my mother perceived she had let her own parents down, I could not. This pressure only grew following Tony's death.

The great news is that there was still time to save myself. I could embrace the beautiful energy that protects caretakers when they finally learn how to include themselves in the mix. Of course, the teacher in me had to turn it into a research assignment, allowing me to not only help myself but to somehow feel like I was educating others on the highs and lows of caregiving.

According to the National Alliance for Caregiving, in 2023 almost thirty percent of the U.S. population acted as caregivers, with up to two-thirds of them being employed in other jobs as well. And would you be surprised to know that women assist with the more challenging tasks such as bathing and toileting? I wonder how many of them ever plan for their own health care, respite, or well-being while doing so?

Care-**taker.** Doesn't mean the person receiving the help is selfish, but I'm wondering about a new term that we all need to embrace: self-**giver**. I'm going to start the self-giver campaign for all of us who have been pouring from an empty cup for far too long. You know the one I mean—the cup with the cute saying "The Joy of Giving" etched on the outside, for us to read while we pour pots of coffee down our throats to stay awake.

I know I never planned for self-care. If I had a list of my most important things to do, my own needs certainly never even ranked in the top fifty. In retrospect, I see how utterly broken my thinking was. I should, indeed, have been the first thing on the list. I'll never be able to apologize enough to my own daughters for being the best role model and the worst role model all wrapped up into one seriously messy package.

Caregiving can ripple its way into a million open spaces and before you even realize it, the words *not now, wish I could, maybe next time, after that, let's take turns* fall out of your vocabulary, along with any good sense you once had to at least *attempt* to find balance between what you give and what you receive in life.

In many ways, I felt like I always filled the role of giving care in my family. My mother called me her "happy" child, so even from a very young age it was proclaimed that I would be the "glue stick" of our gang.

I liked the role. I thrive on relationships, laughter, and yes... attention, so I got the job with fair credentials. But with every year that passed, the role seemed to become a little heavier and heavier. By the time I was caring for both of my dying parents, it was nearly undoable.

I understand how caretakers die unexpectedly before their loved ones, and I felt like I was headed in that direction for the two weeks before my mother passed away. I say this with one-hundred percent confidence: Mom knew it, too, and I believe she decided to die because of it.

She may have been dying but she was no dummy, and she could clearly see the exhaustion and frustration I wore on my leaky face (despite the intense love I had for her). Conversely, I could see the guilt on her face, stealing her pride and making her feel horrible for the tasks I would complete day in and day out, making it possible for her to live for one more minute.

It wasn't uncommon for me to work all day, do the tasks that maintained my own household like walking the dog, making dinner, paying bills, going to the grocery store, followed by doing all the same things for her minus the dog. Some nights I wouldn't leave her place until one in the morning. Happy that I got to see her. Furious because I had no idea how to keep moving forward without completely losing it.

Before she died, I found out that my years of insane sunbathing as a teenager had come back to bite me—literally in the nose. I had to get ten stitches on the right side of my nostril along with a skin graft. I had just gotten to her place after my first bout with Mohs Surgery for skin cancer. It was only a day procedure, but she thought I had been in the hospital for a week. My eyes were black and blue, and I was covered with bandages.

Looking back now, I cannot even imagine the fear she must have felt with her confusion about the word "cancer," thinking that there was a possibility she could lose me, too. Losing one child had been more than enough for her to bear. Her cognitive decline during the last few days was proof to me that life was about to change in big, unknown ways. Reflecting on it now, I believe she had a small stroke shortly before she passed away.

She was, by far, the most intelligent woman I had ever met. I'm quite sure she was gifted, but they didn't "test" children when she was little. And her childhood had been scarred by her early pregnancy at the age of sixteen. Oh, do I wonder what different paths she might have taken had that not happened. But then, there wouldn't be me, either, would there?

We were at the end of the line and each passing moment robbed her of the intellectual clarity that had guided her consistently throughout her life. She was tired. Confused. Worn down. Full of mixed feelings. Faithful and fearful in equal amounts regarding the thought of truly leaving this life to enter the next. If I'm being perfectly honest, we were both fatigued with the entire journey that takes you to the other side.

I can laugh about it now. Couldn't then. But I can now. In fact, I can laugh until I fall to the ground crying. Even after she passed, the caretaking contract had an addendum.

Ironic?

Funny?

Weird?

I don't know.

My act of caretaking would still include a few more items for her transition into her next life to truly go smoothly. My mother was a proud woman. If she owed even five cents to someone, and I did not pay off the debt, I'm quite sure she would find a way to come back from the afterlife and haunt me for all of eternity in increments of five. How in the world could she rest in peace if the bill had not been paid? So began the aftermath of caretaking.

The first job was to go through the apartment—furniture, clothing, bedding, towels, toothpaste, toilet paper, perfumes, important papers, rotten food from the refrigerator. At first my fingers (more my heart) wanted to save it all, and then within a few days, I found myself hurling items into her apartment dumpster without any consideration for what may or may not be valuable. I say that in jest, as I also brought an entire U-Haul full of items back to my home with the chairs that she and my father sat in, her big feather bed, and her china cabinet full of trinkets and treasures that literally dated back a hundred years.

Thank goodness for the God moments like the shell I saved, where her hands reached down from the heavens and said, *slow down*. I noticed a broken conch shell on her bedside table, and I was just about to throw it away when a note peeked out of the curve.

When I pulled it out, it read, *If I ever go away, I will miss you forever, and forever, and forever, and forever.*

Just slow down. It's all gonna be okay, she was telling me. She knew that I would find that note, and I love how methodically she planned it, right down to its placement by her most important things located perfectly by her bedside to comfort her each night.

Seven days it took me.

Seven long days.

For one entire ritualistic week, I cleaned, vacuumed, dusted, moved, threw away, cried, and read letters.

My mother had devoted the entire top drawer of her dresser to saving all the cards we had ever sent her. I was literally shocked when I opened it to find notes that I had written that spanned second grade to college. The birth of my babies, to my late thirties, forties, and even early fifties.

I cried as I read each one of them, my skin covered in goosebumps because I knew I would never be in this space again. I cried because she had saved the past for me, allowing me to be present in the moment, so that I might imagine a brighter future. Again, she wove an invisible string through it all for me, knowing how I thrived on connections.

I had professed my love for my parents in writing repeatedly, and here were the artifacts to prove it, just in case I wanted to doubt myself.

Eventually, I felt a light shining down upon me and a gentle tap urging me away from the meticulous piles I had created, categorizing the top-drawer treasures I'd discovered.

Grief reached down and gently tugged on my fingers. She clasped her hand in mine and said, "C'mon, it's time to go."

"Don't you know I've been preparing you for this day since you were born, when you had to leave your mother's womb? Pay attention, Greta."

"You've had a series of little losses for the past five decades that were your practice run. Nobody wants to be standing where you are, but you have everything it takes to do this. I'm not going to leave you," Grief assured me.

Tears streamed down my face. My chest was tight. My skin was heavy like a weighted blanket crushing my bones. I had been in my mother's apartment cleaning up the aftermath of loss for *seven days straight,* barely sleeping the entire time. My husband called that day and lovingly expressed, "I am ready for you to come home."

As I turned to look back at my mother's last home on earth, I swear to you the most angelic ray of light cast itself upon her floor. The floor where her chairs held a million magical moments. It called to me as if to say, "I will never leave you." I moved my body to stand one last time in each of her defined spaces as I raised my hands up toward the heavens. In through my nose and out through my mouth, my breath trembled as I sobbed and whispered to my own heart:

This is where you felt the sun creep through the blinds.

This is where you sat, writing copious notes in response to your incredible mind.

This is where you cooked and fed your body.

This is the mirror where you found your reflection.

This is the bed where you slept and dreamt of a better world.

This is where you took your last breath and rose up to the gates of Heaven at last to be with Tony and Dad again.

The door clicked one more time as I pulled it shut, and I headed down the stairs that we had first climbed seven years before when I told *her* to start moving. When my father had moved to assisted living, we had to sell their home and move my mother into an apartment. She had broken some vertebrae in her back and didn't think she could climb the stairs, even though she had been healed by this point. I remember telling her, "Of course you can, and you will, and I will help you." I knew she would feel safer on the second floor because in her mind, it would be harder for somebody to break into her apartment.

It was me now. I was the one who had to move, and so I did.

My caretaking words are for the women younger than me who don't even know what lies ahead for them. The ones who watch me and learn from me. Who unknowingly slide their hands to grasp the invisible baton that I pass to them when we turn corners and run like bullets toward our destinies.

Ashley taught me ways to heal myself. I had been a great caretaker for others. So great. But I failed miserably with my own self-care, the very thing I preached the most to others. I remember vividly discussing with her the sadness that surrounded the images I had of both of my parents, so ill and diminishing in their final days.

They were two of the most beautiful, alive, and vibrant humans you could ever imagine, but at the end of both of their lives they were sick and empty. My father's eyes were so black that his pupils disappeared. I knew in his last hours that his soul had already risen to watch over his body.

Ashley taught me how to close my eyes and see them perfectly healed again. After that I had a dream of them holding hands at the airport as they pulled their suitcases toward a new and beautiful destination. Together. For all of eternity.

My new journey was beginning as well. One that would include my own healing and self-care. The start of my self-giving.

WINGS

Keep walking
Until you run
Have faith
Your wings will take flight
And all the weight that you have
Carried upon your shoulders
Will lift you into Heaven,
Where you will be free at last

ASCENT TO HEAVEN

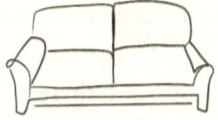

When I was a little girl, we went to church every Sunday. My father was a Methodist minister when I was first born, but that didn't last too long. It was long enough to create funny memories, like the day I crawled under all the pews during his sermon, causing him to stop and beg the congregation to please find Greta and return her to her rightful owner in the front of the Lord's House. Dad's faith and "ministry" never ended, but three years into his service in a formal church setting, there were higher bills to pay, political causes to learn about and lead, and open doors inviting him to think outside of the box. Thus, the way he spread his love and light took a right turn at *You Can Only Do It This Way Avenue* and *Greater Possibilities Lane*.

Our family continued to dip in and out of services over the years, but then a minister would refer to "burning in hell" in some form or another, and we would find ourselves back at home making pancakes and nourishing the alignment of our mind, body, and soul. Our language was love. It was cemented by faith and belief that a greater power watched over us. We knew that our lives were driven by purpose, and that trusting the universe to guide and protect us would lead to only good things. Things that we could utilize to help ourselves and help others.

As a small child, I used to lie in my bed screaming up to God in my loudest most articulate voice. For goodness sakes, Heaven was so very far away! I was quite sure that if I did not make myself known in big ways, He would not hear my needs, therefore rendering Him unable to deliver the correct responses to my prayers.

Hello, God, it's me, Greta! Can you hear me?

My parents would laugh as I shared "lists" of things that our family and the world needed. Of course, I'm pretty sure some of it was self-serving as well. *If it's not too much to ask, Lord, I could use the 64 pack of crayons, please. I've got some pictures in mind. And have you seen those new markers that are scented? Like, wow—those are cool! I could write a letter to Grandma if I had those. It would be nice if we could get some food and clothes to those in need as well. And, by the way, I need (would like) a new pair of shoes, too, please.*

When I grew older, I took a religion class at the University of Florida. I got so immersed in learning about world religions and would envision a council of love leaders sitting at a huge table, surrounded by clouds, collaborating on how to love and lift all the creatures of the world. Christianity. Judaism. Buddhism. Islam. Confucianism. Hinduism. Taoism. Only a few of the potential beliefs a person could hold. Who was I to determine that somebody else's convictions were not equal in value to mine?

I have no doubts that Heaven exists. That I am in line to get there. And that my brother, father, mother, and all the loved ones I have lost are strolling around past pearly gates that lead to lush gardens and flowing waters surrounded by their friends and family. Joy and peace are carried by the most beautiful breeze. I am perfectly fine with living there in my afterlife and would sign an after-lifetime lease with first and last month's rent if that were required.

So, why am I so afraid of death?

"Grief, get over here. We need to talk. You've done this to me!" I accused.

"I can't help how you process this. I can only stand by you while you do. It is you who must do the work," Grief said.

"Oh, Grief!! Easy for you to say. One minute you seem to care, and the next I feel like you are planting seeds of confusion in my head."

"You, my dear, are the master gardener."

She wanted me to take responsibility. I get it. But Grief had done a number on me, whether she would admit it or not. I certainly do not think about my own death all the time. I can happily state that my life has been so full and rich with love, family, friends, and experiences... but then there is that "two percent of the time" that holds the part of me that fears my own passing. How silly, I know—but I worried about my daughters and my husband being left with my unfinished grief. It reared its ugly head on the anniversaries of those who had gone before me. When I turned twenty-eight (the age of my brother when he died), I was sure that I might die, too.

And so on. I thought about dying at seventy and seventy-eight (Dad and Mom respectively), and I would calculate the years I had left with my family if that was to be my ending point. Because I became a mom at the age of thirty-five, I would literally cry imagining my daughters being so young without me when I die. *Will their children know me?* I would wonder.

I know this all might sound crazy to you, but Grief was guiding me to the place I needed to be. Right here. Right now. This second in time. My knowledge, grace, and understanding that, in fact, this is the only minute that matters, and my ability or inability to live in it to the fullest is my job to figure out. Not hers.

"Maybe it would help if you thought about your ascent to Heaven," Grief nudged.

"I don't know if I'm ready to do that."

"Just try," she softly encouraged. And she placed her hands atop mine, just enough for me to feel the warmth running from her energy into mine. Like freshly baked cookies rising to open lips awaiting a treasure, I longed for her wisdom.

I lowered my gaze and closed my eyes. Engaging all my senses, I surrendered myself to the deepest rivers of my mind to imagine a glorious journey that would wait for me until it was just the right time.

Cool mornings with the sun peeking through the trees to warm me will always be my favorite kind of days. They lead me back into my childhood years at 445 Stockton Drive in Baton Rouge, Louisiana. There some of my favorite memories still reside. The huge magnolia tree that engulfed our front yard danced in the breeze, carrying the enticing scent of the oversized blossoms that consumed our entryway. The minute my feet stepped onto the sidewalk, a hundred lizards scurried in all shades of green and gray to find their destinations. I wound my way around to the backyard that held our greatest outside play and conversation. I can still hear the chirping of the beautiful blue birds that called our live oaks home.

My feet were almost always bare, so I had to move with great care to avoid the stinging caterpillars and acorns that were abundant in springtime. My parents had built the most beautiful, rectangular red brick patio underneath the sweeping canopies filled with moss. It was large enough for a patio table and eight chairs to house family and friends for backyard feasts and social gatherings. The smell of coffee and the sound of sweet musical notes hung like a backdrop for the stage that awaited our performance. The terra cotta and earthy red tones were barely visible due to the countless plant varieties that grew into a border that turned this space into added square footage for our small home.

Things seemed so simple then. We played "H-O-R-S-E" with the basketball hoop and held ping-pong championships under the covered driveway. The hose was our savior on a steaming hot day, reminding us of the juxtaposition of all of life's feelings—hot and cold, good and evil, happy and sad.

What meant the most to me then was love. It was the only thing that mattered. I didn't sit around wondering about what I would eat that day. I didn't worry about how I would pay bills. I never looked at the porcelain smooth skin on my face and gave thanks for the absence of wrinkles. I didn't ponder about what outfit made me look the thinnest. I didn't question whether or not I was good enough. I didn't fear taking chances with the hurl of my basketball and didn't cry if I missed the shot.

Quite the opposite, in fact—I jumped for joy when I heard the swoosh of a perfectly landed ball. I knew exactly where to place it within the invisible "square" I had created in my mind that assured the ball would land inside the net. I loved watching the sun go down, and I pretended that it was a huge peach disappearing into the ocean. Perhaps more importantly, I took the time to pay attention to the magnificence of it all, instead of rushing toward meaningless tasks that really don't add value to my life.

"Grief," I gulped.

"Yes, dear?" she soothed.

"I think, before I enter the gates of Heaven, I would like to walk past my childhood home. One last time, I'd love to smell the aroma of the magnolia flowers with the warm sun shining down upon me on a fresh spring morning. I'd gladly feel the tickle of a bright green lizard tripping over my bare feet as the cool water from the hose rinses them. Before I enter Heaven, I'd throw the basketball one more time and glance back at my favorite brick porch to the sound of the ball swooshing through the hoop, because I made it. I made the shot!"

"Then, that, my love," Grief affirmed, "is exactly what we shall do when the time comes."

THE PRINCIPAL who I work for is one of the most amazing women I know. She is fearless and focused. She makes everything appear effortless, when I know in truth she works tireless hours to orchestrate millions of unshared decisions with others. On top of everything that she does as an outstanding leader, she runs marathons, most times waking up at 2 a.m. to commit herself to weeks of training to improve her skill level.

But here is the cool thing. She also manages to find time to stand along the race course to applaud other runners. She has shared with me the psychological benefits of having somebody who just cheers you on.

In a weird way, that is what Grief did for me. She encouraged me. She stood on the side watching me not give up. She led me further and further down the road toward the greater enlightenment I craved and counted upon like I needed oxygen to breathe. Grief knew the path was going to include dips in the road, elevated surfaces, cracks to avoid, smooth sailing at times, and a finish line that called to me. She encouraged me to pace myself for the long haul because that was the only way I was going to make it all the way.

CAUTION

First responders never wait
They hardly even hesitate
Hands so weary
Heads so full
But nothing dulls the forceful pull
They slowly droop
If careful not
To fill their ever-loving pots
Be cautious of the very start
'Cause in the end you'll fall apart
Left alone and wondering why
The caring felt like one big lie

FALLING APART

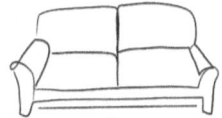

By the time this is published, I will be close to sixty years old.
Writing this book has been the first time that I have allowed
myself to completely fall apart, releasing all the thinking, habits,
feelings, and actions that do not serve my best life.

Oh my God. It was so hard, but at the same time, the most
amazing act of love I could have ever given myself. Pouring these
stories onto the page ripped off the Band-Aids that had been
covering my wounds. I knew that sharing these details would invoke
strong feelings, but I had no idea how intense my memories
would be.

You see, holding your grief inside can create a plaque that builds
over decades, preventing your healthy flow and limiting your ability
to move freely through all that you are and want to be. It will reroute
the electrical impulses of your heart if you are not careful, leading to
ablations for remapping the emotions you have allowed to lose their
proper rhythm.

Having been a surviving sibling, I also dealt with the fact that
my brother's death became the core of who we were as a family. My
grief, as I have stated, became secondary to my mother's. Don't get
me wrong. I understood this at a much deeper level once I gave birth

to my own children. There could be no greater feeling of loss than the "out of order" disappearance of your own child. It didn't make sense. Not supposed to work that way. How do you bounce back from that one?

But for me, Tony's death shot me into a trajectory of constant overachieving. I couldn't bring my brother back, but I could do everything within my power to please, perform, and perfect what we still clung to as mother and daughter. The pressure was invisible, but I felt it. And when my father was diagnosed with early-onset Alzheimer's, instead of disappearing this invisible pressure transformed into other crushing responsibilities. This lasted for thirteen years, followed by another seven years of caretaking for my mother, who became so weak at the end she weighed under seventy pounds.

I love the Japanese art of putting broken pottery pieces back together with gold. I'd like to think of my year of falling apart as the first real opportunity I had to rebuild into an even more beautiful version of myself—embracing my flaws and imperfections, inviting the shimmering strength to assist me in reclaiming my power.

I imagined a light so bright that I could not stand it. The light was inside of me, and I was ready to let it shine throughout the entire world around me.

I recently had an amazing opportunity to meet an up-and-coming social media star who goes around interviewing strangers. He asked me about love and loss, and I had answers for it all, but true to form my statements were controlled. No tears ran down my cheeks. I gave lessons of life, summarized in my natural teacher format.

Meeting him and performing my "trauma dump" (as my oldest daughter Julia referred to it) was impactful. Unlike me, Julia was still able to reach inside to her deepest registry and find her tears. For a brief moment, I longed for my own tears. I missed the days when they could flow so easily. I missed the days before my wise mind kicked in, striving to be the gatekeeper of my deepest feelings.

Julia apologized for crying as his gentle voice soothed her, giving her permission to be herself. "It's just that listening to my mother—well, it reminds me. My grandmother was my person. She listened to me in a way that nobody else could. Loved me like nobody else could."

In that moment, I felt the brightest light possible, knowing that my Julia was one in a long line of strong women born to change the world with their love. I also knew that Grief had been to visit her in the same unexpected fashion that she had visited me. As Julia and I departed together, I knew that my mother was walking alongside us.

Where is Grief leading me now?

"For God's sake, Grief, I don't know how much more of this journey I can take.

Haven't I fallen apart enough for you? You should be writing a book about me. Not me for you. You act like you are the expert of me. Stop throwing my fears in my face!"

"Patience, Greta," Grief asserted. "I promise you can trust me. I really do have your best interest at heart, you know."

We're looking down upon a hospital bed—but this time, it is me who is lying there. Tubes and beeps abound, softly expressing an impending departure that belongs to only me. Grief slowly directs my attention to the vision of my own departure.

My girls are on one side of the bed, standing over me hand-in-hand with tears streaming down their faces, their father on the other side.

Beep.

I'm trying to speak, but the words won't come out. Do they know that I can hear them?

Beep. They tell the nurse to make me comfortable. "We don't want her to be in any pain."

Beep.

I'm fine, I'm trying to tell them... why can't they hear me? *Somebody listen! Don't wait. Don't wait to do the things you want to do...*

Flatline.

No more chances. No more seconds. No rewinds or redos. The breathing ends and I am gone. My girls begin the same ritualistic goodbye routines that I, too, once performed. Scene over.

"Well?" Grief sighed. "What did you see? What did you hear? What's your take-away?"

"They, too, will have the day that I once faced, and I will hear and feel them just like my mother heard and felt me. How fitting that I am trying to plant the same message into them that my mother tried to grow in me: *This is your big, beautiful life, and your time on Earth isn't going to last forever. There's never going to be a 'perfect' time to do the things you want to do. You will be tired. That's normal. You will fall short with the bills at times. That's okay. You will love work one day and want to call out on another. Do it! You look great in those pants but not so much in that dress. Have a laugh about it. You'll feel like you don't have enough time for something because of all of your responsibilities, but you can make the time! Stop cleaning so much and make more messes. For every laugh, there will be a cry. And for every tear, there will be a smile. Let yourself feel. Let yourself play. Let yourself believe that it's ALL okay. Essentially: Don't wait to do the things you want to do!*"

Grief smiled and nodded. "You're getting it, Greta. Keep up with this and you just might have a good story to tell."

I FOUND myself back on Ashley's couch many times over the next five years. This time it was only reserved space in my mind, for Ashley had long since left hospice and started a private practice, and I couldn't afford to follow her.

It was amazing to me how quickly a day had turned into half a decade without my mom. I looked more and more like her each time I stared into the mirror and remembered a Halcyon Days box she had gifted me once that read, "Mirror, mirror on the wall, I am my mother after all."

I began to laugh as I applied over-the-counter retinol to what the facial lady called my "lines of expression." No wonder the grooves ran so deep. She had no idea the intensity of my emotional release over the years. My face was a roadmap for a million trips, all leading to the depths of my heart.

Ashley had helped me breathe through the contractions of pushing my mourning out, giving birth to a more vulnerable me. One who anticipated, expected, and welcomed grief. One who knew the purpose and the power of grief. One who modeled and spoke freely about grief. One who felt somewhat missionary about normalizing grief, so that others could be free to feel it too, instead of trying to stuff it inside or avoid it. I was an ambassador for the "club" and the initiation into its secrets.

Falling apart to my core had now secured me the final badge of honor that I needed to fully understand the intensity of grief's gamut.

DEFENSE MECHANISM

She pressed an invisible button
Meant to ignite her protective gear
That would save her from flying objects
Aimed at her caring heart—
Denial Bubble Activated

DENIAL BUBBLE ACTIVATED

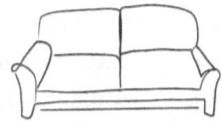

It's ironic that in my current field, I spend all my days and nights pensively lost in the analysis, reflection, and celebration of all feelings, because if I honestly look back upon my life, the only true feeling I ever really liked was "happy."

I wasn't sophisticated enough in my younger decades to recognize the variance in words like *joyful, cheerful, elated, ecstatic* or *melancholy, depressed, anxious,* and *exhausted.* I pretty much felt either *happy* or *sad.*

My childhood memories fall within distinct shades of emotion, but making a T-chart of "happy" vs. "sad" could have easily covered it for me at the time. Birthday party: happy. Having to go to daycare so mom can try to work: sad. Friends spending the night in seventh grade: happy. Moving to Florida for my dad to take a new job: sad. All gains and losses could be effortlessly filed away on one side or the other.

I think the ability to activate my denial bubble started at an early age, so by my early twenties I was an expert at denial. Do you have a denial bubble, too? They're really quite nice as far as defense mechanisms go. Lightweight. Low cost. Easy to carry around with you to the various settings you encounter. Invisible to the eye so as not to clash with your appearance.

The times you would expect me to be sad—holidays, birthdays, traditions—are not always the times that melancholy hits me. Although I must say, the taste of spinach dip at Christmas (my father's favorite treat), the smell of my mother's Chanel No. 5 perfume, the touch of the leather case my brother used for his camera, the sound of a household full of family members gathered around a Thanksgiving table just about to share gratitude for the past and hope for the upcoming year brings a wild rush of sensory overload like none other. The memories are beautiful and tricky all at the same time, sometimes invoking sadness and other times tears of great joy and gratitude. My senses are so mighty in their ability to breathe life back into someone whose body has long disappeared.

While the years following my great losses fully activated my denial bubble, my insatiable hunger for healing was also alive and kicking—leading me to many pinnacles of discovery. Denying my sorrow had turned into an incredible talent for avoiding pain, but I also began to appreciate the power in understanding the necessity of life's peaks and valleys.

In the valleys, I began to bathe in the water of my own tears, cleansing myself of all that was holding me back from mending my broken heart. My light began to shine brighter with each recognition of "mountain top" moments, the ones that taught me the definition of elation. Countless cheerful celebrations made up a list longer than the losses. My wedding, moving into my first home, changing lives as an educator, the births of my beautiful daughters, adventurous vacations, laughing with friends until my cheeks hurt. I trusted the necessity of feeling both the ups and the downs to fully appreciate the joys that I had previously taken for granted. I learned to appreciate the co-existence of sorrow and joy.

I will always keep bubble-wrap in my self-care kit to act as a barrier against the most intensely painful moments in life, like the night the rise and fall of my father's chest stopped, and the world as I knew it ended. Cheyne-Stokes breathing is something only people in the club know about. The slow, irregular rise and fall of your loved one's chest, warning you that the time is coming soon for their breathing at last to cease forever.

I'll never forget the night my father sailed into the night and over the stars to find his wings. My eyes deceived me, and I couldn't believe that his chest was no longer rattling like a rollercoaster traveling up and down the track. I wrapped myself as tightly as I could in bubble wrap and, for at least thirty minutes, laid upon his broad shoulders to *prove* to myself that he wasn't breathing.

Surely this was a mistake. My father was meant to live forever.

Grief looked over at me as tears rolled down even from her experienced eyes. Every now and then, the pain got the best of her as well. With a gentle nod of her head, she soothed me with a look of affirmation that said, *Stay there as long as you need to believe that your father's last breath is, in fact, the air that is holding you up right now.*

HURRY

Up and away
For two weeks
And a day
Catch her fast
While you can
She'll flutter away
If you stand

BUTTERFLY WINGS

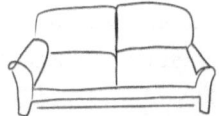

Twenty-one thousand days ago (and a few extra), I started living. Forming, transforming, metamorphosing from infant into toddler into girl into woman. After almost six decades, I marvel at my butterfly wings protruding from my back with perfect symmetry, each covered in the iridescent colors of red, black, and yellow, reflective of my life experiences.

Just like my flitting friend, I learned to hide from predators camouflaged in my patterned cloak when necessary. Most times now, I am brave enough, tenacious enough to lean into the light; quickly fluttering by if you aren't paying attention.

Is there a mark in the road, I wonder, where living turns to dying? The average lifespan of a butterfly is two to four weeks. How could a life so beautiful feel so short? Does attitude, mental health, belief, or one's spiritual base contribute to its quality? One of my dearest friends shared the most beautiful quote by Benjamin Franklin with me that she heard upon the loss of her best friend at a very early age: "A long life is never good enough, but a good life is long enough."

I suppose I have always been a "liver," but I have also witnessed the pain of those who believe they are dying just a little bit each day.

My mother was one of those people, so perhaps that is why her actual passing left me paralyzed in grief. She had been preparing me for her death for years—and yet, when it finally came, I felt so unprepared.

I feared my own death. Having my girls at an older age did weird things to me. I knew how right my mother was when she said how much I would miss her, and I cried thinking about my daughters sitting together holding hands and crying when I died. Do you ever wonder how you will die? Will it be the long, drawn-out journey that I had with my father, or will it be a death like my mother where the last two weeks of her life felt like a shooting star slipping away from me at the speed of light?

Or will it be like my grandma? She sat silently in her chair that was literally about twenty feet from her mailbox. A huge picture window standing between her and my grandfather who went to check the mail. By the time he returned, she was gone. No warning. Angels had snuck into the house and quickly carried her home.

Grief had an odd way of bringing me gifts each new time she came to visit. I wasn't as scared anymore when I opened the door to greet her face. She walked through the door like an old family friend at this point. She brought a coffee table book entitled *Butterflies*. She placed the book in the center of the table, and I immediately turned to the contents which read:

- Understanding the Seasons of Life.
- Appreciation and Gratitude for Everyday Things
- Self-Awareness
- Growth Through "Hard" Times
- How to Share Experience and Empathy with Others
- Acceptance of Our Own Mortality
- Insight into Loss
- Gift of Caretaking
- Search For Self-care

I wasn't quite in the mood to start reading yet. It seemed kind of long, but I liked flipping through the pages, as if to prepare myself for a great series that was about to captivate me and hurl me into binge-watching each episode until the grand finale.

I've always been inspired by a friend who often talks about "doing the work" and "doing it with fear." I watch her commitment to working through difficult things in her own life with tears of admiration in my eyes because I know the courage that she possesses and the calling that she has to build strength in others.

Grief work must be done despite the fear that it can invoke. Fear of feeling. Fear of loss. Fear of moving on to joy that exists when tears begin to dry and light begins to shine on fresh, new possibilities. There is an incredible gift that comes with loss if you allow yourself to magnify the details.

I will always love unexpected visits from my mother the most— the visits I least see coming, but somehow are perfectly timed to when I need them the greatest. She sails toward me on butterfly wings, reminding me that I am safe and ready for the rebirth that awaits me.

FOLDED

I'll never forget my father's hands
And the way our fingers folded together
Building a bridge from his heart to mine
Making me believe I could cross over all paths
I needed to travel to find myself
Home again

MY FATHER'S HANDS

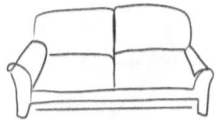

Losing both of your parents is strange. It leaves you feeling like an orphan. You meander back into memories of your nuclear family, but with them gone, it all seems so small now.

My sessions with Ashley focused so much on the loss of my mother, but the truth of the matter is, I was a Daddy's Girl. If there was, indeed, a cookie cutter that produced children as replicas of their parents—that would be me and my dad.

We moved the same, looked the same, talked the same, laughed the same, connected with people in the same way. It was as if we shared a brain. Since he's been gone, there are still many days in my life that his voice travels through me as a legacy of all that he has left me.

I'll never forget my father's hands. They were strong and his fingers were thick. Those hands led me, lifted me. They read books to me and pushed my bangs away from my eyes so that I might see life more clearly. They took me to musical theatre performances, wiping away my tears when the talent was so overwhelmingly magnificent that I broke down.

Those hands played the baby grand piano and wrote 800-page proposals for work. They joined mine to hold hymnals at church. I still can't sing in church without bawling my eyes out, because those moments belonged to my father's hands.

Those hands cooked pancakes for me every Sunday and gestured emphatically when there was a life lesson to be shared. *Listen up* those hands would say.

Those hands picked up Roald Dahl's *Charlie and the Chocolate Factory* and turned every page at the dinner table one night, reading the entire book in one sitting as my brother, sister, and I literally begged for "one more chapter, one more chapter!" instilling a love for reading in me as I was lost on a chocolate river sailing into my imagination.

Those hands sent me three dozen roses when I broke up with my first love, such a visual representation of the things to come in my future; the big and beautiful burst of love that awaited when I thought I'd never love again.

Those hands moved me from high school to college and college to my first-year teaching and living solo to walking down the aisle toward my husband. Those hands pulled my babies from bathtubs, wrapping them like tortillas in warm towels before playtime, where those hands created castles out of building blocks, magical and faraway places for my children to explore.

Those hands held the phone, listening to every joy and every sorrow that I ever knew, sending truth and wisdom back for me to catch in my own hands.

Those hands taught me how to help others. They held real and metaphorical signs in marches against social injustice or in moments of inauguration.

Those hands held my hands when he lay in a hospital bed after finding out that he had early onset Alzheimer's, followed by doctors creating cocktails of prescribed pharmaceuticals that made him crazy. The trial and error of combinations seemed only to contribute to the perception that he was slipping away from us faster than our efforts could control. They didn't know him. They didn't know about his capable hands.

Those hands passed the torch to me as I gently began to do the things for him that he had done for me my whole life.

After my father died, I laid in bed for at least six weeks before I said even a word to my husband. I tucked myself beneath the heaviness of my grief blankets, convincing myself that I must have cancer or some terrible disease. My bones literally ached and kept me up at night. My neck and upper back constantly reminded me of their exhaustion. *We can't keep holding your thoughts up,* my spine cried.

How could the universe be so cruel? How could I now be faced with the long road of my own ailments on the heels of my father's passing? I was horrified that there was something seriously wrong with me.

Perhaps I would even rather die myself, slipping silently into the night like the moon disappearing when you turn a corner on a long and winding road, no longer to be seen. My hips and my thighs ached each night as I slipped the vessel called my body into the bed that would taunt me with insomnia.

I made an appointment. You know the routine. Primary care first, so you can get a referral to a specialist, and then to my surprise two paths emerged: physical therapist and rheumatologist. I began the exercises and evaluation that would assure the therapist that I had rheumatoid arthritis or lupus.

All the signs were there. Let's just confirm it with bloodwork. The rheumatologist walked into the office as I nervously awaited the news that would verify the new course of my life.

"You don't," she said. "You don't have either one."

Suddenly, I was the seven-year-old girl faking a sore throat in the school clinic to get the hell out of school, so that I could spend time with my mother.

Have I made this all up? It feels so real. What is she talking about? She doesn't know me. She doesn't know how real this is and how much I literally ache at night.

At that moment, I surrendered to her expertise. I recapped the literal anguish that my body is speaking. And instantaneously, there she was. Revealing herself in full costume. Standing tall in her midnight-black regalia. My girl, Grief.

"So, what do you think it is?" I muttered to my physician.

Grief gave me a little wave.

"Grief," the doctor replied. "It will bring you to your knees."

I began a regimen of stretching, exercises, and sacredly attempting healthy sleep habits. Twice a day I swallowed turmeric to counteract the inflammation throbbing in my body, reminding me of the loss that I felt. I learned to sit with it. I can only imagine what my mother felt inside of her bones the day the sheriff knocked on our front door to bear the worst news she would ever learn in her entire life. The day they came to tell her that her only son would never return home from work that day.

In fact, he never made it to his shift that day. By the time friends had called to check on him several times, she was already preparing herself for the reality that something tragic had happened. She positioned herself at the front door, waiting. Waiting for the confirmation that would rob her heart forever.

What did *her* body say that day? Heart pumping, ears numbing out any words other than "There's been a terrible accident." Knees collapsing, body falling into the arms of my father. Adrenaline rushing to fists. Fists banging on his chest. Voice rising. Screaming empties the horror onto the ears of listeners afraid to speak.

"Bring him home!!!! Go and get him. Bring him home!!!!"

Time freezes. Stomach churns. Feet ache. Mind wonders, *How will I go on for one... more... second?*

Her life would be gauged in that moment by the number of seconds she now had to live without him. 1,009,152,000. And what do you suppose held her up?

My father's hands.

Receiving the news, eleven years later, that my father had early onset Alzheimer's was the worst joke my mother could ever hear. It would be the onset of more grief for her. More delayed grief for me.

The anticipatory grief for my father became a familiar friend constantly inviting herself over to the house. I hated the way she showed up unannounced. So rude. I cried rivers of tears just thinking about what I was losing, so much so that the day he actually died, not one drop fell from my eyes. To this day, eleven years later, I still have not cried for my father.

Instead, a river of grief for him runs through my veins.

My grief for him was so debilitating that I had to create a dam to block the rushing waters that could potentially destroy me. I control that dam to this day. Every now and then it budges, tries to move with a trickle of beckoning, pleading me to come nearer to my loss.

But I can't, and I won't. Not yet.

My father's famous saying was, "Don't push the river, it flows by itself." I must believe this will guide me until the day the dam breaks and I float away in the direction that calls for me.

I have one picture that I go to frequently of my father, holding my first-born daughter when she was a baby. You cannot see his face in the picture, only his hands.

I'll never forget my father's hands.

UNDERWATER

What sound do you hear
when you begin to drown?
When you feel yourself sinking deeper
into a trance
surrounded by the arms of a riptide
tugging you downward
toward a force
greater than you have ever known—
Do you hear anything at all?
Or are you lost in the
scream of silence?

PERFECT LITTLE PAN

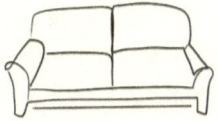

"Mom! Meemaw is asking for morphine," my daughter cried. "You have to come home!"

My God. I thought I was ready for this.

She had been dying for the past thirty-five years.

I was sure she was a cat with abundant lives, born again each time into a more complex and enticing version of herself. After all, she had lived through the loss of my brother in a head-on collision with a semi-truck, cancer, broken hips, my father passing from early onset Alzheimer's, a suicide attempt, COPD stealing her every breath. Two hundred pills were not strong enough to counter the strong will to live that ran through her veins. No matter how hard she tried to escape the pain of her own life, it still captivated her. Her contract went longer than expected. There was work to be done, and she was the only woman for the job.

"I'm on my way," I replied to my daughter. Half-empty with the disbelief that sand could actually stop pouring through the timer that endlessly seemed to mark our time together on this earth.

Grab your keys, tell your boss. Drive on autopilot, not knowing how you get to your destination but trusting your mind to know the way as you begin to play the movie in your head called "Us."

I remember the day we made pumpkin pie together like it was yesterday. I had all the "small" versions of her baking tools. Little spoon, little bowl, little pie pan, little mixer. "Only bake from scratch," she would insist, measuring each ingredient to perfection. The smell of pumpkin and vanilla extract. God, that smell. Her knife slowly caressing the flour as she smoothed the top of her measuring cups before pouring the love that would embody "pie" into the same ridged, sky-blue bowl that we would continue to use for the next fifty years together. I still have that bowl.

The door opens as I swing my purse and keys onto the closest chair. *Where is she? What's happening? This is too fast. I'm not ready.* We had agreed it wouldn't happen this way. We were still planning to have the "two-week talk" that she had with her own mother, where both retreated from their normal lives to discuss all that mattered in life plus bonus questions, my mother and her mother finishing the same way they started—together. Just the two of them. The mother and the daughter, bound by an invisible force that only mothers and daughters know about. A secret sorority, minus the bullshit. Okay, probably full of more bullshit.

My pie is done! All of the same ingredients from my mother's mixture—canned pumpkin, eggs, sugar, cinnamon, nutmeg, salt, piecrust—condensed into a smaller version for my child-sized dish. At age five, this may very well be the biggest moment of my life. I grab my masterpiece that must be shown off immediately to my father, but as I am running, I slip. The pie goes flying out of my hand, out of the pan, strewn across the floor like lava as tears erupt from my eyes. **Nothing can fix this moment.**

I rush to her bed, like I always do. She knows the routine. You sit up first. Ground yourself to make sure you are not dizzy. We don't want you to fall again. That's it. First wiggle your toes into your right shoe. There it is. C'mon. Do it. She starts slipping. You wouldn't think that sixty-seven pounds of human flesh and bones would be a lot. But in this moment, she slides away from me as I realize she is already disappearing from this life and into the next.

My pie! My pie! How can I ever live through this loss? My mother's loving hands nuzzle me while she gently scoops up the ingredients and nonchalantly smooths them back into my perfect little pan, like this kind of thing happens all the time to master chefs. My dad is beaming as if it is the ultimate desert. **She knows how to fix everything**.

What's going on? Why does this hurt so much more than Dad? I feel like I am having surgery without anesthesia. Is it because this is my last parent dying? Somebody get the manual. I need a crash course on how to do this correctly. Time is slipping. Warm tears are pouring down my face. Can tears have a fever? Because if they can I am sure mine are on fire. Call hospice back. They will know. It's their job. *Keep her alive*, I think.

"Your mother is dying."

"No, you don't understand," I plead. "She is just slipping. I can't hold her. I need help."

"She has defied all odds," they continue.

I'm sinking. Sinking lower into the water. Running out of air. My brain feels dizzy as the air bubbles slowly dance above my head that is spinning, spinning, spinning. I'm losing consciousness, and I smell the warm delicious scent of pumpkin pie and vanilla extract.

Did I give my mother the morphine yet, or did I unknowingly take it myself?

I can't do this. Not yet.

I promise this time, I will stop doing the dishes and cleaning the house if you promise to stay alive long enough to have even one cup of coffee with me. On the porch like you always ask when you beg me to just sit down with you. We will shut off the oxygen, and I swear not to tell if you devour one more cigarette while we laugh uncontrollably about some silly memory or throw things at the

television, channel-surfing between MSNBC and CNN. Or I
know! Let's listen to "The Prayer" by Celine Dion and Andrea
Bocelli, dressed in our imaginary gowns as if we are attending a gala
performance. Let's feel the notes so deeply in our souls that we hold
hands while we watch the video, pass the tissues and cry like babies
together. You want a piece of pie? I brought this great pumpkin pie
over. We can put homemade whipped cream on it. All made from
scratch, of course! Only "real" whipping cream and confectioner's
sugar with a splash of vanilla. I chilled the mixing bowl and the
whisk first for you.

The hospice nurse makes it to the house, but only for
instructions that I do not want to hear. "Go ahead and start the
regimen of around-the-clock morphine. It will keep your mother out
of pain. She will go peacefully. We can't stay tonight, but we will be
back first thing in the morning to help support you."

I'm so tired. I can't keep my eyes open anymore. My lids slam
down like hurricane shutters, prepping for the storm ahead. This
has been going on for weeks. But I must stay awake. I can't miss one
second of her living! Why is the sand moving so quickly now?

I need to tell my mom that the remote only works for the
television. It doesn't run the microwave. And the skin cancer I had
last week was benign. It was only a day surgery. "I know you
thought you didn't see me for a week, but quite the opposite—I was
here until one in the morning each day after working nine hours *and*
feeding the dog."

I curl up next to the shell of my mother. My girls run to get her
favorite umbrella that, when fully opened, depicts Michelangelo's
Sistine Chapel from the inside looking up. "Meemaw, let's take a
trip to the Vatican City," they say as both them slide under her arms,
already resemblant of angel's wings, revealing the masterpiece with
a press of a finger to open the parasol. She knows they are there.

I am fading into sleep. The hours pass.

Now my girls are gone. The sand is gone. Just me and my

mother. The way that we started. Only the mother and the daughter, bound by an invisible force that only we know about. In total darkness, I pop up out of a deep sleep at 3 a.m. to the sound of *utter silence.*

Who will scoop up the ingredients and smooth them back into my perfect little pan? ***Nothing can fix this moment.***

SURPRISE

Be open to treasures
That hide if you're not looking.
The sparkle will catch your eye
When you least expect it.
Accept the gift.

DUSTY, OLD BOY: THE UNEXPECTED CHAPTER

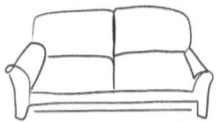

We all have unexpected chapters, don't we? You know. The ones we didn't see coming.

Or maybe we did, and we just didn't want to acknowledge it.

Here is mine.

My husband and I both grew up with multiple dogs. We were "dog people." Dog lovers. Dog enthusiasts. When we first got married, we had two of the most beautiful fur babies. Ranger was a regal German Shepherd, a solid and stunning mix of tan and black, gifted to us by my husband's parents who were downsizing. He watched over us like a six-star general, and Zach—well, he took the prize! I'm quite sure my bias prompted me to claim this fellow as **the** most beautiful purebred Cocker Spaniel you could ever lay eyes upon. His ears covered in silky, soft curls dripped down to the ground like cascading waterfalls, and his soul, well—his soul was as deep as the doggy ocean.

Ironically, the loss of my brother prompted my possession of this precious pup. My parents arrived at my first apartment after I graduated from college with baby Zach in tow, a caramel-colored creature of comfort that fit perfectly within the palm of my hand. I instantly fell in love with my very first "all by myself" dog to have and to hold until death do us part.

If you asked my best friends at the time, they would have told you, "She's crazy!"

Zach filled an empty space for me, and I literally took him *everywhere*.

"I feel separation anxiety if I'm not with him," I confessed to others.

So, he became my right-hand man traveling to and from my parents' home, activities with my friends, and all my adventures in between. An intense connection between the two of us kept me feeling safe and secure and gave me a positive focus during the height of my family's grief, and for that I felt grateful.

Zach loved me as much as I loved him, and neither of us really needed anybody else to fit into the mix. I didn't realize it at the time, but I had decided: *Human love only ends in heartache and disaster, so I'll kindly avoid all that potential pain by remaining single. I will never ever hurt again like I did the day my brother died. I will secure my heart with a double-bolted lock and a "Do Not Disturb" sign.*

"Zach, you are the only one who deserves my love," I convinced myself.

By the time he was eight years old, and I was thirty-one, I was living alone perfectly content as a "dog lady" who may never have another boyfriend again.

Shortly after, another tragic accident took place. Princess Diana died in a speedy traffic collision that took her glamorous and meaningful life way too soon. Immediately, pictures and videos of the car crash inundated the media, and that is when my nightmares began. Ten years of suppressing my brother's accident began to bubble up like an overflowing pot of scorching water on the front stove burner, leaving me scrambling for potholders.

What I may have failed to mention earlier is that a professional photographer passed my brother's car wreckage on that fateful day.

Camera in hand, he decided to capture shocking images of my brother ejected from the vehicle, lying on the side of the road with almost every bone in his body broken. This photographer then proceeded to mail them to our home. We believe he thought our family might try to sue the truck driver, and that he was looking for an opportunity to make some cash. Yes, I did see them all, and no, I've never been able to forget them. So, the images of Princess Diana's accident became a silent reminder of my own trapped grief.

As a result of my disturbing dreams, I turned to a professional counselor for the first time since my dear school confidante who had helped me analyze my initial year of dreams. This counselor helped me delve into some tough questions about my life. Did I really want to be alone? Or did I have too many unresolved notions about love barricading my ability to build connections that went deeper than a rain puddle? Was love even real, or did it equate to control? Control over me, under me, and through me but not from me. All my boyfriends in the past seemed to have the upper hand as I willingly took the back seat, and our family life following my brother's accident revealed anything but composure or mastery of our actions.

In only five short sessions (the amount approved by my insurance company), I declared that I no longer needed the services of a licensed mental health shrink, and I subsequently met my current husband (and love of my life) Chris. My therapy take-aways were:

- To have love, you must be willing to take risks again. It's worth it.
- Being a surviving sibling is a niche all its own. You don't have to feel guilty for living.
- File the photographs of your broken brother away and turn off the television. On second thought, just throw the photos away completely.

I began to live my beautiful life with one caveat in the marriage contract:

"I die first. Agreed?"

One nod of Chris' head sealed the deal.

"Okay. Good."

Ranger, Zach, Chris, and I found two years of love and laughter before "Raney," as we called him, suffered from severe hip pain and had to be put down. Shortly after, Zach followed his lead, leaving me devastated, staring Grief in the eye for having the audacity to infiltrate people *and* pets! For three weeks my body trembled with sorrow, aching for the return of my first-born son, Zach, but nothing could bring him back to me because he was gone forever, like my brother. For six months, I would walk into the front entryway upon returning from work, swearing I could see his body curled in a ball at the top of the stairs, his luscious, long ears blanketing his big brown eyes. But he wasn't there—just the illusion of his presence remained.

Once more, I followed Grief back into the club for a meeting:

"I WILL NEVER LOVE ANOTHER DOG AGAIN ENOUGH TO FEEL PAIN. PERIOD. DID YOU GET THAT?"

Grief agreed that animals can cause as much pain as people can.

Chris and I proceeded to have two delightful daughters who filled our lives with joy daily. Mom, dad, baby girl number one, baby girl number two. No dogs. Just kids. Dogs have such short lives and make you cry when you love them too much.

This worked out until my oldest turned ten and my youngest celebrated her eighth birthday.

It happened so unexpectedly. I was teaching first grade when Cheryl, the mom of one of my favorite students, entered the classroom. Burrowed in her elbow rested the brother of my current and most beloved dog, Dusty. The minute I laid eyes on the mini-dachshund puppy, I knew that the time had arrived to purchase our first family dog with the girls.

For eight long years following Zach's passing, I couldn't bear the thought of losing another dog. I adored Ranger, too, but Zach was MY first baby and everything about him represented the era of my life following my first huge loss. But one look at Dusty's brother left me asking a million questions:

Knowing the unconditional love that a dog provides, how can I not give this experience to my own daughters?

What else teaches kids better responsibility than caring for a pet?

How much would it cost?

How will I tell Chris?

I could feel my adrenaline amping up, and before Cheryl left the room, I had a time set up to meet my new puppy. The minute I laid eyes upon his tiny little nose and paws, his dapple-colored fur, and his expressive eyes, it was over. The transaction took place, and I wrote out a check for three-hundred dollars. Worth every penny.

Step number one involved choosing the perfect name. We debated between Oreo (due to his dapple-colored fur that looked similar to an Oreo cookie in some spots) and Dusty (because he was covered in multi-colored patches of white, black, and light brown as if he had been dusted by those paint colors). All family members got to decide their preference, and Dusty earned the overriding vote!

He arrived at our house just in time for my youngest daughter's eighth birthday party. She decided it would be fun to "marry" Dusty for her party, so all of her little girlfriends dressed in their Sunday best and lined up as bridesmaids as Jaclyn exchanged vows with our new pup. This was just the beginning of fourteen years of wonderful memories all revolving around our beloved buddy.

He went on family vacations with us like our trip to the Biltmore in Asheville, North Carolina, where he roamed through the gardens chasing butterflies. In our backyard, he dropped his body next to the cold, soft grass for back rubs and regular basking in the sun. He sat upon our laps for every movie and snuggled at our feet for every festive gathering, praying for small scraps of delicious "people food" to fall into his tummy. He always made me laugh with his bath time "zoomies" and his hysterical Dachshund "side eye" (doxies can be somewhat judgmental) or the way that he would take just one of our shoes ever-so-gingerly in his mouth to the other side of the room just because he could. He didn't chew it or destroy it. He simply felt empowered that he could move it to another place of his choosing. We were so joyful as a family, and for a moment in time, I forgot that dogs have a heaven, too.

Fourteen years later, my oldest daughter, Julia, lives successfully in her own apartment with a great job and amazing boyfriend, while my youngest is living at home finishing her degree at the University of South Florida. Jaclyn's love for Dusty only intensified as the years progressed. He was, indeed, her little brother, following her everywhere she went in the house, especially when I was at work or gone running errands. Jaclyn worried about his health and saw firsthand the slowing down of his systems.

Prompted by Jaclyn's keen observations of Dusty—she noted the rapid growth of a mass near his tail area—I began to concede to the fact that something might really be going on with him. Like all old dogs, Dusty had gotten bumpier and lumpier along the way, but this was different.

"Mom, you have to call the vet!" Jaclyn insisted.

I was able to get Dusty in the next day, yet still I expected to hear that it was a fatty tumor or something of the sort. The distinct smell of the vet's office with the dander of cats and dogs merged with the familiar sound of the office parrot and his crisp "Hello, hello, hello!" alongside the warning sign "Do not put your fingers in this cage. He bites!"

Dusty and I slipped into room number three. The room smelled strongly of rubbing alcohol, and in the background I could hear barks and coughs and the jingle of leashes adorned with tags that rang like bells of beckoning. I gently placed Dusty on the cold, stale silver examination table that reminded me of the night my mother tried to take her life and her small frail frame lay upon the same surface as we waited in the emergency room together for somebody to breathe life back into her body once again.

I loved my vet's office, and I trusted them. They took a conservative approach to care that I appreciated. I didn't feel like they were taking advantage of me. They spoke to me honestly, as if they were treating their own animals. I guess that's why it felt so serious this time.

"I'll need to borrow Dusty from you for a minute," the tech informed me.

I gave Dusty a quick kiss and she whisked him to the back for a closer look without me.

Upon her return, she notified me that the vet would be in soon to discuss what he saw.

"This mass feels a little different. I'd like to do some x-rays if you're on board. Wanna see if there is anything in his bones."

"Of course!" I replied.

I waited patiently before another tech appeared, sharing with me that the vet was tied up with another "complicated" case and would be with me soon.

Shortly after, I found myself staring at x-rays that revealed an enlarged liver, a massive, dense growth in Dusty's abdomen and the results of an exam determining an additional mass in his colon.

Jaclyn had been right. Little man, "Moo" as she like to call him, had a finish line, and we were learning about the details today. Right now. Too soon. Not ready.

I went home and shared the news with my husband and daughters and sat in solitude for a while, absorbing the fact that Dusty would soon join Zach at the gates of doggy heaven.

Dusty crawled into my lap as he always did, but this time felt different. I was suddenly, painfully aware that our number of cuddles had a stopping point. My dappled, darling dachshund would enter the pearly gates just like all my human friends had, and it would hurt with the same awfulness their losses had.

Perhaps some would not understand that one could feel the same intensity of loss for an animal as they do for a person, but I did. At this point, it was only Grief, in her anticipatory form, once again asserting her power over me. Dear God, she was powerful.

It felt so contradictory to come home from the vet to happily receive an email from my editor that my book—this book—was almost done, polished and shiny. I was on my last round of revisions, thinking how ironic it was that my old buddy's visit to the vet led to me to one more glance at Grief's face before handing my story over for final delivery.

Grief decided to nestle on the couch beside me, leaning in to the warmth that Dusty and I created together upon the comfy couch that had been declared his bed, propped up by oversized pillows and countless blankets.

"Can you believe it, Dusty? We did it, little guy. I'm almost finished with my book."

His hazel-brown eyes stared back into mine as if to say, "I never doubted you. You've always done what you set out to do."

"You made it easier, Dust. Thank you for believing in me," I responded.

"I've watched over you for fourteen years, and I couldn't have asked for a better mom," he returned.

"And you have been the perfect son," I completed.

"It's been a great run," Dusty said through his deep and distinguished stare. "I'll never leave you, you know."

"You'll think of me when the sun hits your own skin with just the right angle in the backyard garden as you walk the path that we shared together."

"Yes, I will," I sweetly nodded as I reached out to feel his silky coat.

My hand slowly caressed Dusty's long spine, taking extra care not to exert pressure upon his sturdy back. Dusty had seen it all. He'd been there for all of it. And each time I returned home, he was, indeed, the first to comfort me. In my grief, his silence spoke volumes. He didn't interrupt. He just listened. He knew what I felt without words needing to be spoken the night I crawled into bed after leaving my father's empty body. The day I finally returned to my home after my seven-day tribute to my mother, it was Dusty who silently soothed my tears.

The night I received the news from the vet, I fell into bed, spooning Dusty's tiny little body. Had he been my spirit guide, sent to bring me the strength I needed to survive loss? In his own sweet way, he had gently reminded me, over and over again, that life is for basking in the sun, rolling in the grass, burrowing down unknown holes, and wagging your tail so briskly and enthusiastically that your bottom just might fall off.

Grief sat down on the far edge of the bed. She patted her lap and Dusty crawled upon it, only to fall fast asleep. She looked over at me and whispered, "He was worth every minute, my dear. Wasn't he?"

LISTEN

Mourning Has Broken
High
Low
Which way will you go?
Rise with the sun
Sink down with the moon
Your answers
Are waiting
To speak to you
Soon.

GLORY IN THE STORY

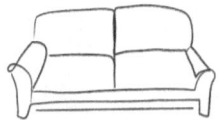

Could you believe with me for a second that Grief had something good to offer me? Perhaps there could be some gift in the stories that were strewn together throughout my losses? Loss became one of my themes, a small mark of who I am as a whole entity.

My girls still laugh at me sometimes and tell me that I am the best little griever they know. "You are unbe-*grievable*, Mom!" they will giggle. My commitment to understanding grief and the quest to heal myself and others does at times bring laughter to our house. I'll admit there is some eye-rolling. But it is all good. Don't we need these bits of humor to balance the intensity that grief brings?

The impact of my previous losses will always make goodbyes seem just a little bit harder, a little more dramatic. I'll never forget dropping each of my daughters off at college and literally feeling like I could not breathe without them for the first few moments as I walked away, leaving them to navigate their new adult lives. Thank God I knew the strong moral compasses tucked inside their pockets, leading the way.

When I left my father in his first assisted living facility, it felt no different. We decorated his room, met roommates, and toured the facility as if he were beginning a four-year program at a university—the one that would earn him his last degree and a certificate stating, "Well done, my faithful servant!"

The pain of loss can feel like death by a million cuts, but then there is the glory in our stories. The darkest moments somehow shed a brighter light on the steps that lead to our victories, our chosen "favorite" memories, the pictures that make the scrapbook of our existence.

And dear reader, a part of my stories will always be linked to yours as well. It is not just gravity that keeps us grounded. The universality of our walk on Planet Earth—which, for all of us, includes loss—pulls us with an unavoidable force back to the ground upon which we must walk to move forward. Like my mother after my brother died, I wanted to float away from my sorrows by pretending they weren't real—but I knew in order to truly heal I had to confront the real pain, and to do that I must stand still in its presence.

I believe our stories are always being written in real time, with a constant, steady flow of editing and revising; redirecting and rerouting to find our happiest pathways marked with the brightest light. As we walk through our sorrow, we must also look for the beautiful signs of life blooming all around us.

Recently in a book club, I led the group in a reflective exercise to create a dream team of individuals to support them on our earthly journey. Without thinking, I assumed they would pull from their living family, friends, and colleagues, but one beautiful soul in the group added her late father and a deceased professor who had played a huge role in her doctoral dissertation.

Why not? Why not! I perked up. Why not add our heavenly helpers to the list as we envision and remember their ways and their words and the magical talents they harnessed, helping us believe we can handle all things. I found so much comfort that day in this reminder that just because a human body may be gone from our vision, the presence of all that matters remains intact. *Ahhhh*. Now I understand why my parents wanted to include Saint-Exupery's excerpt in my brother's service: *It is only with the heart that one can see rightly. What is essential is invisible to the eye.*

Every time a friend loses somebody, I lose myself a little bit more in their grief, sometimes crying even harder than the actual family at funerals as my husband squeezes my hand and whispers, "*Breathe.* You're being too loud!"

I can't help it, though. I can't help it because I *know* their pain. It reminds me of my own pain, but it hits me even harder because now I imagine somebody else who I love deeply having to endure that same feeling, and I desperately want to take it away from them.

Thank God for the day Brené Brown came into my life, helping me truly see the point at which my "empathy" crosses into the danger zone, and I no longer know where I end and the other person begins. (Thank you, Brené!) There must be a healthy connection between my caring and other people's personal journeys that have nothing to do with me.

We all must stand alone in our grief for a time.

Grief has stamina and determination, and she will sit beside you for decades until you are willing to acknowledge her. I didn't want anybody to know she was there.

Yet, she was there. She was with me. All the time.

Hiding beneath the surface of my appearance like an extra layer of skin.

She camped out in my backpack.

She dared the right person to pull the smallest pebble able to release the dam that protected me. Whether it was a small trickle or a sinkhole depended on the size of the stone removed. It could be as simple as me feeling overtired after a long workday, or as intense as watching a friend face the agony of her own mother's passing. My emotional overflow followed no regulations.

My pebbles jiggled when my guard was down. Overwhelming

loss snuck up on me when I was in the kitchen alone making my mom's famous Christmas date cake. As I sifted the dry ingredients into the satisfying cream of butter, sugar, and eggs, the smell of vanilla and cinnamon made tears gather in my eyes. The overwhelming sweetness of the dates mixed with chocolate chips could win awards. I remembered her gentle hands "pretending" to slap my fingers away from sneaking a taste that would turn my lips into candy.

In the background, we always played music. My mother and I would listen to the beautiful notes and lyrics and literally cry at the talent of others. At the end of her life, we shared so many precious breaths singing those songs together.

Pull the pebble back, quickly. Push it hard. Lodge it in. This cake must be ready for when our company arrives. The sound of her angelic voice whispered in my ear, reminding me, "Clean as you go. It will make it easier to get everything done before company arrives."

And then the piece de resistance: as I slid my mother's Christmas date cake into the oven, her song—our song—came on the radio. What were the chances? *The Prayer* by Celine Dion and Andrea Bocelli. His rich, crisp notes complimented her upper register as I gave in to my own tears and let the dam break. My entire body broke out in goosebumps and I knew my mother was with me in that moment.

For so many years, I wasn't ready, willing, or capable of handling Grief, so I pushed her under the radar to survive my life.

I was too young to understand the complexity of my family's grief after my brother first passed away. If my agony lasted for more than sixty seconds, I found a way to file it inside the bulging mental folder named "Later."

Sometimes, I wondered how my life could have taken such a drastic turn. I wanted my parents back. The ones I grew up with. The ones who laughed and lit up the room with their incredible energy and zest for life.

The people who know you best will speak to your silence. With them, it won't matter that you are unable to find the right words to share what you are experiencing. Watch their eyes and let them in. Sit with them in the dark. Tell them your stories. Repeat yourself if need be. But remember to laugh too.

Despite the great sorrow that my father's Alzheimer's journey brought, there were also days that we laughed until our bellies ached. My dad had lost a ton of weight, and I will never forget knocking on the door to visit one day. My dad opened the door and his pants immediately dropped to his ankles. We laughed until we cried!

Toward the end, he could not leave the house without getting anxious and wandering, so we found a way to meet most of his needs within our home. I learned how to cut his hair, and he would gesture to his right and left and say, "What about them?" I practically opened up a business as I began to give his imaginary friends haircuts too. He would tell me about family members who had already passed who had come to visit him for the day. "How wonderful," I would reply, and mean it.

He would light up like a starry night as he explained to me that he had been out in the forest all night, cutting down wood to make treasures for my mother. Like a magic genie, he generously granted anything I wanted. "Anything at all," he would say.

Would you like a new car? Done!! It's in your driveway waiting for you right now.

Want a new TV? Done!! It's waiting at your house.

Sometimes, I would need to sneak back home to take care of my girls, so I would tell him they needed my help with their homework. Guess what Dad would say? "The girls don't have to do their homework. I've done it for them here." Boy, didn't they wish that was the truth!

He paced the halls of his new home, thanking the other residents. I fondly remember him pointing to another woman with

Alzheimer's and telling me how he had to thank "this little lady" for all that she had done with him to gather toys and school supplies for children living in poverty. His excitement bubbled over as he described televisions, video games, stuffed animals, books, paper, pencils and the lot all waiting in gift bags to be dispersed. The only place those two had been together was the dining hall, but she graciously smiled and returned with a, "Well, you're welcome!"

Laughter must be found to endure this journey, along with an awareness that there are others who deeply care, who are ready to comfort you when you are ready to share. One of my mother's favorite poems was by Emily Dickinson:

Hope is the thing with feathers,
That perches in the soul.
And sings the tune without the words,
And never stops at all.

In the face of my deepest sorrow, I can still hear my mother's voice reminding me that hope does not disappoint. She commits. She shows up. She delivers. She encourages. She believes. She lifts. She finds glory in your story.

LET HER IN

Despite my attempts
To lock her out,
She found the open cracks;
She knew the mighty
Hacks
That only wisdom bears
When someone hides their greatest cares.
The irony was hers to see:
Her entry in would set me free.

MOURNING HAS BROKEN

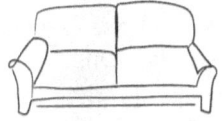

S he was *my* grief.

    For my eyes only.

Designed specifically for my growth, pain consumption, and ultimate release. At first, I double-bolted the door. Windows covered with boards to prevent damage from the inclement weather. Items from the yard safely stored at the front of the house to prevent gusts of wind from pitching them into the open cracks and unprotected corners.

Over time, I began to accept that Grief had been with me the whole time. She was the first one to hold me when I was born—that first loss of being pulled from the warmth and comfort of my mother's womb, into a cold and foreign world that would carry me further through the ups and downs and all-arounds of love, loss, and life.

Grief had been there preparing me the whole time with the little losses. I just wasn't aware enough at the time to realize it. Now, I needed to let her lift me with the wind and trust that I would land on a solid surface. Better yet, I needed to sway in the direction of the breeze with a firm belief that my roots were strong enough to hold me in place.

Grief knocked gently at first, a polite solicitor. Then her ways became more sneaky, a trickster attempting to break-in, but I was much too wise and guarded for that. Trust had schooled me in the past, warning me of incoming strangers such as she. I knew how to block Grief at the pass. For years, I thought I was winning by meticulously compartmentalizing my grief stories into folders filed away in my emotional safe box.

But my game plan was all wrong. I thought I had been able to avoid saying goodbye to my brother, best friend, grandparents, mother-in-law, and father by activating my denial bubble time and again. That bubble was big. That bubble was fiercely protective. Unfortunately, it did not stop the pain; it merely delayed and compounded the pain.

So, it was time. It was time to let Grief all the way in. It took me all this time to realize that she was my shelter for the category-five storm that swirled in the distance.

My mother dying felt different. It was as if a thirty-five-year sentence was up. My own grief came dashing out of that emotional safe-box where it had been hidden for decades. It whirled out with tornado force strength, and it did so with a vengeance.

I was finally free of the distractions that had prevented me from feeling my own true loss. Beginning with my college graduation immediately following my brother's passing, I had launched into a series of milestones all worthy of my attention. My career, my marriage, my daughters—all such joyful chapters of my life. But in conjunction, there were many diversions that were destructive to my healing. The long journey of my father's early onset Alzheimer's, followed by my mother's health issues, and my work in a high-needs school gave me all the excuses I needed to negate my own pain. No self-awareness of my own trauma existed. In a profession where I served as a loving, protective presence for others struggling with triggers, I failed to recognize my own adverse life experiences and the very real consequences that came with them.

Grief waited and watched. Listened and learned. Gave and took. She sat on the other side of a perfectly designed see-saw, expertly facilitating my rise and fall into the present moment.

The present moment.

Let me say it again...the *present* moment.

My thoughts began to wander like they often did when I was meditating. The goal was always to stay focused, but like any normal human being my mind would stray into the forest, over the branches, toward an opening in the sky, grasping for the light that was breaking through the trees.

Thoughts.

Thoughts.

Thoughts.

I repeated this to myself to pull back into the present moment that I was so desperately trying to live in.

But here comes Grief for one more blast into the past.

Oh, Grief. Sometimes I still don't know whether to hate you or admire the hell out of you. Here you go again, shoving me into the time machine that so willingly catapults me back and forth in time.

My mother and I are sitting in the chairs nestled on either side of the table that held my father's glasses. We're having one of our last conversations, seasoned to include life lessons that need to be learned and burned into the important wrinkles of my mind for later reference like super files—all this wisdom condensed and consumed as quickly as possible before she's gone.

"Listen carefully, Greta. We're almost done. One more visit back to your mother, but this time you need to just sit in silence and listen. I mean really **listen**. Hear your mother's dying message," Grief whispered.

My mother's eyes seemed extra green this night. I honestly have never known even one other human with green eyes like my mother. Like soft-spoken emeralds, they stared through my soul with a regal vibe that only a few are lucky enough to experience.

Her slender hands, covered in veins transparent enough to reveal the blood that ran from her DNA bucket to mine, clasped my fingers tightly, pulling me closer toward her then-beating heart.

Beat.

"Listen to me."

Beat.

"Don't wait to do the things you want to do."

Beat.

"Do them now."

Beat.

"This is your life."

ONE LAST PHOTO from my childhood slipped from Grief's loving hands into my own. In it sat my perfect little, nuclear family on a couch. A couch just like Ashley's. We had everything we needed for a lifetime of beautiful memories together. The world was waiting for us with abundant joy and laughter.

"It was never about endings, Greta." Grief smiled.

"It's about beginnings!" I proclaimed.

She leaned into my heart and softly whispered, "Go get some."

THE BEGINNING

Hands together
Head bowed down
Words fall slowly
On tired crowns
Body lifts
Words comprised
Help your weary bones to rise
Open heart
Healing starts
Hope will show
To do her part
Prayers are answered
In their time
Believe, believe, believe
In mine

AFTERWORD

I'm not an expert on grief.

I'm not a licensed mental health counselor.

I'm not a grief counselor.

I'm simply a woman.

I'm a human who has experienced quite a bit of grief in her lifetime. Born to another woman who suffered tremendous loss that in turn impacted me because I was the daughter who adored her, seeking to please her at every turn.

I was a daughter doing the best I could for a daughter (who happened to be my mother) who was doing the best she could. It wasn't until she died that I truly felt permission to feel my own grief. I tiptoed around hers for decades, wishing so fiercely to protect her from ever feeling one more second of pain after my brother died.

She pleaded with me to work through my own grief while she was still alive, but I wasn't ready. I am so blessed for the counselors, family, and friends who stood by me during all those years of loss, allowing me to grow into the woman I am today: Grief's child.

Thankfully for me, my mother and I had the beautiful gift of being able to spend her last moments lying next to each other in the same bed. The way a newborn baby lies upon her mother's chest as she takes her first few breaths in this world is the same way that my mother left this world—but this time, it was she who lay upon my chest, taking her last breath.

I believe that she knows the grief work I have done in the past four years, and I can only imagine the pride she feels knowing that it is my mission to pass this important work along to others.

DENIAL BUBBLE DEACTIVATED.

ACKNOWLEDGMENTS

The birthing of this book is due in part to many incredible and special people in my life, and so I must acknowledge that with abundant gratitude.

I would like to begin by thanking my exceptional parents who live eternally through the words that flow from my working brain into my hands, heart, and mouth, and the desire that I host to continuously make this world a better place because of that.

To my sister, who is my longest standing relationship, and the one who has walked the longest road to light with me through the ups, and downs, and all arounds that life offers us daily as siblings. I thank God for knowing that we needed each other to do this life, and I love you with all my heart for being my rock and sounding board.

To Chris, Julia, and Jaclyn, you are my perfect little family, despite all our "perfect imperfections". Thank you for surviving the ripples that come with somebody who is holding grief inside of them. Thank you for making joy the overriding switch to pain and for inviting me to laugh and dance and sing many more times than I cried.

Thank you to my brother, to Hilary, and to all the loved ones who passed from this world into the next so much sooner than any of us could anticipate leaving us to grow and glimpse up into a sky that holds unlimited knowledge of our purpose, passions, and permanence in this world.

Thank you to the inspiring women that I have written alongside in the masterfully cultivated Thriving Authors Writing Academy led by the talented best-selling author and book coach, Dallas Woodburn. The countless hours of conversation, workshopping, and emotional support felt more like therapy than a writing community, and it changed me for the better in ways I'll never be able to express.

More thanks to Dallas (and her team of elves) for not only living their own rich and meaningful lives as a model to us all, but for somehow finding the time to work around the clock to bring other people's dreams into this world. I stand in awe of your ability to empower others to tell their stories in hopes of creating a tsunami of love that takes over our hearts. Our world needs you to lead others toward the space that exists between what was and what could be.

To Doris, I thank you, for being the model of what a rich, long life of service and friendship can and should be. You are and always will be my one and only "giving lady".

Thank you to hospice for magically connecting me to Ashley and to Ashley for placing me front and center on her couch.

And finally, I want to thank my dear friend, Grief. You didn't give up on me when I needed you the most. You, alone, taught me that life-even if it feels too short-is a gift to be treasured and honored beyond all others. Live it each day as if it were your last.

GRETA'S GRIEF WORK

Below you will find some of my favorite grief work activities that I learned from Ashley. Engaging in these exercises over time brought great comfort to me as I hope they will for you.

Take Me to Your Timeline

When I first met Ashley, she asked me to share my first memory related to grief with her. This led to me constructing a timeline of my grief. Through this process, I realized the small losses beginning in my childhood that led up to the big ones like my brother's accident, my dad's Alzheimer's, and my mother's long journey with health issues. Seeing the visual of these events made me realize how resilient I am. It also reminded me that all people have a series of small and large losses strewn together throughout their lifetime. If we're lucky, they don't all happen at the same time. Together, we find ways to support and lift each other up again until the passage of time brings feelings of healing. My timeline helped me see how strong I am.

Happy Birthday Letter

I missed my mother so dearly. Sometimes it made sense when I missed her like her birthday, but other times it seemed to hit me out of nowhere. I remember writing a letter to her on her first birthday after her passing. Ashley sat and listened to every single word as I cried my eyes out, but it felt so special to speak the words anyway. Somehow, I just knew my mother could hear me all the way from the gates of Heaven. Try writing a letter to your loved one. It could be for memorable events like birthdays and holidays, but it could also be the simple pleasures you miss sharing. You may not be able to see them, but I believe they can still hear you.

Journaling

I like to refer to my journaling as "healing through feeling". Because I am a creative, expressing myself through words, poetry, and artwork is tremendously soothing to me. I bought blank sketch books and drew pictures, wrote letters, made collages, captured quotes that resonated with me and so much more. I was able to share this process with some girls at the school where I work who had lost their moms too. The first year after my mother died, there was a very special little girl named Rose with whom I connected instantly. We met every Wednesday and shared beautiful stories about our mothers at the picnic tables. For that moment in time, we were both able to smile again during our most intense feelings of loss.

Ritual Walk

My mother and I both loved the outdoors. I love to walk, and she could always be found rocking in her chair on the patio, sipping on coffee or iced tea, surrounded by luscious plants. I turned our love for nature into a ritual. Each time I went on a walk, I gathered some kind of beautiful stone. Upon my return home, I found a special location in my garden to place my memory rocks until it became a wonderful collection.

Healed Again

Both of my parents were extremely ill. It was so ironic-my father's body was as strong as an ox, but his mind was deteriorating from Alzheimer's. My mother, on the other hand, was as sharp as a tack mentally, but she only weighed 67 pounds and had the end stages of COPD. She literally looked like a paper doll. I was so sad after she passed away because the only way I could envision my parents was in their "sick" version. They had been such vibrant and energetic life forces for the majority of their life, but I was left with these images in the end. I'll never forget Ashley asking me, what would it take for you to see them healed again? We worked on a guided visualization, where I was able to quietly close my eyes and see them young and healthy again. Now, when I picture them, that is the vision that I cling to.

Love is in the Legacy

My father and I shared an intense love for learning and teaching, presenting and supporting, interacting and connecting. There are days that I know his legacy lives through me when I literally feel like the sound of his voice is coming through my mouth. So cool to be able to feel like I am his eternal voice. For my mother, I have now written two books. She believed there was no power stronger than words, and I agree. How might you honor your loved ones? Actions, words, creative expressions like art or poetry, planting a garden, visiting a long-desired destination and leaving a remembrance?

This is only a sampling of the many ways that I honored my grief by giving it a place to be heard. Reaching out for professional counseling and support can be lifechanging as well.

PICTURE PERFECT

This is my mother as a small child, like Fern from Charlotte's
Web, *saving her runt named Snooty.*

Here you see my mother's father, Vernon, with the cigar that always hung from his mouth eventually leading to esophageal cancer.

My mother is perched upon my grandmother's strong shoulders. My nanny carried a lot of weight for our family forging a line of very strong women to come.

My mother is pictured here only 17 years old with a beautiful baby boy named Tony.

My sister and my brother were so close in age. They almost looked like twins.

This is my absolute favorite picture of my father as it shows the deep connection between the two of us.

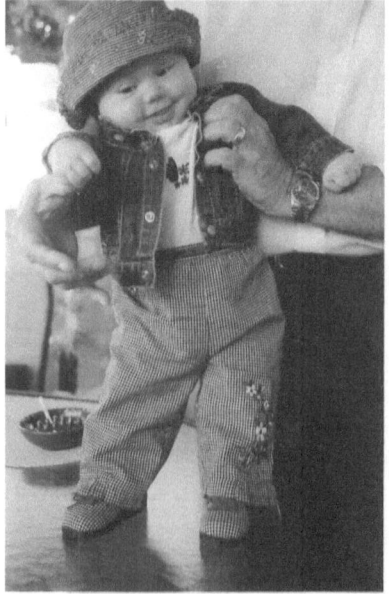

This photo highlights my father's hands holding my first-born daughter. Oh, how I remember the power of my father's hands!

Pictured here, you see the antique washstand that remains in my home as a reminder of the strong women in my family history.

This is my grandmother's antique recipe box that houses the golden-brown recipe cards like my mother's famous Christmas (date) cake.

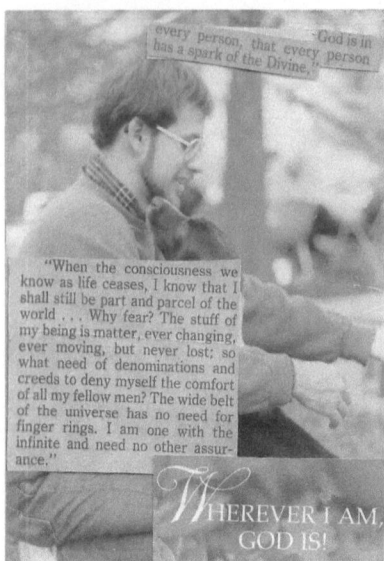

*This picture of my brother hung on my mother's refrigerator for
over 30 years after he passed away, and now it hangs on mine.*

*Once upon a time, there were five of us! I'll never forget the joy of
being alive with all of them.*

Me the morning of my wedding.

I had the honor of being a bridesmaid in Hilary's wedding.

My husband with my daughters creating beautiful family memories like carving initials in his Poppy's tree.

My "little man" and the love of my life.

My first "all by myself" dog.

Me and my best friends' college graduation.

Big brother showing me the world.

Hugging Mom and Dad.

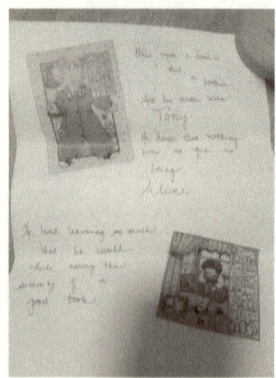

Remembering Tony.

AUTHOR'S NOTE

Dear Reader,

Thank you for taking a chance on this book.

My dream for you is that you or somebody you love deeply is beginning a journey of healing.

I pray that you are surrounded by a million angels sent to somehow ease your pain and lead you to a place of love and light as you travel through your grief work.

Your story is special, and I want to hear it. Feel welcome to reach out to me at:

https://www.facebook.com/gretathemindfulmentor

https://www.instagram.com/themindfulmentor_

ABOUT THE AUTHOR

Greta writes about topics that resonate with her own heart. She dreams of a world where people feel comfortable exploring their personal narratives, feelings, and healing journeys. Her work life spans over 35 years and includes great stories about teaching, speaking, and mentoring others. At home, you will most likely find her in the backyard garden laughing and dancing with her husband, two beautiful daughters, and her darling dachshund. Her first book was written to support the greatest profession she knows, that of an educator. It's called *S.O.S.: Survival Guide for Teachers Old and New*.